FAITH ADVENTURES
Volume One

Can God's Unsearchable Riches be Discovered

NORMAN SERGENT

xulon
PRESS

Copyright © 2016 by Norman Sergent

Faith Adventures Volume One
Can God's Unsearchable Riches be Discovered
by Norman Sergent

Printed in the United States of America.

ISBN 9781498492591

All rights reserved solely by the author. The author guarantees all contents are original and do not infringe upon the legal rights of any other person or work. No part of this book may be reproduced in any form without the permission of the author. The views expressed in this book are not necessarily those of the publisher.

Unless otherwise indicated, Scripture quotations taken from the King James Version (KJV)–*public domain*.

www.xulonpress.com

FORWARD

F aith Adventures-Volume One-Fifty Episodes

Stephen Manley's Endorsement

> "Faith in Jesus is not a mental or theological state; it must flow into our daily living. You will want to participate with Norman on this adventure of faith."
> Stephen Manley

Stephen Manley has pastored for fifteen years, traveled worldwide as an evangelist for forty years and has established Bible training centers in more than twenty-five countries. Stephen focuses on preaching, discipleship and pastoral care and is the author of twenty books, including commentaries on the books of Matthew and Acts.

PREFACE-DEDICATION

First, and above all, I want to thank God for inspiring me through His Word. Upon hearing His voice giving me the remembrance of the ten episodes from my childhood and adult years before Christ changed my life and forty episodes after Christ. One of my pastors had taught about how God was working in our past lives unknowingly, which I never forgot. God, from the very beginning, had me writing things down for many years. Within the last ten years, He has inspired me to write many things and I have sent many emails out to my friends. The majority of believers have responded back very positively, without one negative word. Here are some of the readers' feedback that have only read a small portion of the book Faith Adventures:

"Your stories are wonderful and truly engage the reader and I believe you have a gift."

"You are a masterful story teller and the reader can relate with your stories."

"Your writings are very encouraging and your voice conversational and very friendly."

"Your writings are authentic and honest, which is rare today and speaks to my heart."

"Several ministers said preparation was needed in their life to finish strong the race."

"Your stories have cleared up a lot of confusion in what I have heard in Christianity as a new believer and through your writings God has shown me I'm called to be His disciple."

Some of the readers that God gave me told me that I write very well, but I write too much. I sought the Lord on this matter and prayed. If that's what they want, then I will give them short stories. These are my true life stories, and how God interacted in my life for some time without me knowing it. Once He changed my life; I knew it had been Him doing all these things from the beginning. I didn't know this was going to become a book until I began writing it. I believe God had me write this under the inspiration of the Holy Spirit and God has made me the "pen of the writer." (Psalms 45)

I want to thank my family for always supporting me in the ministry God has given me pertaining to God's Kingdom. Again, I give thanks to a young man named Gary, a man of integrity who taught me many things pertaining to the computer. Also, I want to thank a wonderful young woman named Jen, full of God, for partially editing my book to get it started in the process of publishing it. I also want to give thanks to Word-Weavers on learning to be a more effective writer and encouraging me always in critiquing my book.

Faith Adventures Volume One

INTRODUCTION

Faith Adventures is about how God demonstrates His interventions in our lives through the circumstances throughout our lives; even when we didn't realize He has been working. Have you ever thought in going back in your thinking, how exciting it could be to rediscover your childhood? Many of us have seen movies that would take the characters back to the past and we have been captured by these, only to realize these are fantasies. Manifestations that God brings are real live events. These events that come to mind can reveal to us how God was working on our behalf, doing things within us that have made us a good part of what we are today. I have come to the realization this is not only possible, but highly probable. When we have seen, and experienced the wonderful works that God has performed in our lives; we can come to the realization that nothing is impossible with God.

Believers that truly have the Holy Spirit residing in them can tap into the things that most would think as mysteries, but to the believer walking in God's will, they are matters that God can reveal to us before Christ and even more so when we have totally surrendered our lives to Him. Our Messiah Jesus, said one of the most profound things that you will ever read in the Scriptures. John 15:14-15 says

Ye are my friends, if ye do whatsoever I command you. I no longer call you servants, for the servant knoweth not what his lord doth: but I have called you friends; for all things that I have heard from my Father, I have made known to you." (NRSV)

Is it not just a little thing that God could do in revealing things to us that we have long forgotten? I truly believe God has had me write Faith Adventures, not only to tell my testimonies, but to demonstrate how God can speak to the reader to rekindle those thoughts that would be helpful in them to gain a greater appreciation for what God has done. There have been great things God has done on our behalf and the enemy desires to erase these out of our minds. When we have victories that we can look back upon, these can spurn us on to greater victories.

When you read, this book take notes on how God speaks to you. I read a book many years ago that has impacted me to this day. One quote I shall never forget; "People that write things down retain 75% more than those that don't."

Only God can awaken in us the truths we need to hear and see. That profound thought or event that God is bringing to you, could be once again be lost forever. You will read my childhood in the first ten episodes. Not all of my childhood experiences will be revealed because some of the events would be too painful. God spares us of these events, unless He wants to take us back only to bring us further forward today in our walk with our Lord.

The next forty episodes begin with our new life in Christ and how God wants to work in our lives to bring us to a place of the purpose He has designed for our lives. There can be many trials and tests and I know from my experiences, God will get us through if we just learn to trust in Him in everything that comes our way, day after day. Everyone's cross is different. This is why He said in Luke 9:23, "And he said to all, if any man be willing to come after me, let him deny himself, and take up his cross daily and follow me." (NRSV)

I prayerfully believe that as you read how God wants to work in our lives, hearing His voice and staying sensitive to the Holy Spirit; we can begin to have an understanding of the life of obedience. According to Hebrews 5:8- 9, "He yet learned obedience by the things which he suffered, and being perfected, became the author of eternal salvation to all that obey him." (NRSV)

This book is in response to many things I have written to the Body of Christ. I have always endeavored to be an encouraging voice in this world of discouragement. The response of my readers about two years ago was that I was writing things that were good, but too much for most to read. I prayed about this, taking this matter to God and I felt led to give the believers what they were requesting. This is how Faith Adventures got birthed, not knowing from the beginning it would become a book. I'm a new writer, but I believe I have much to offer to the believers today because many have commented positive comments that they would like this entire book. This is not because of me, but the Christ that is living in me daily to produce these true to life memoirs to this day. God willing, there will be more volumes of Faith Adventures to come.

Faith Adventures Volume One

Table of Contents

1.	God Imprints in My Life Before Christ	15
2.	The Blizzard that Blew Me Away!	19
3.	Rationalization Catches Us in its Trap	22
4.	False Seed of Religion Keeps Us from Real Relationship	25
5.	Relationships in The Flesh Can be Deceiving	29
6.	Joey Clarke: My Nephew's Story-Gone into Glory	33
7.	Mom's Faithful Prayers	37
8.	God's Calling Could Be Unknown	42
9.	God's Deliverance from Being Prejudiced	46
10.	Beginning of Faith Impartation- Unbelievable	49
11.	Life in Christ After Being Born Again!	53
12.	New Expectations with Little Faith	57
13.	God's Plan Nothing Less than Miraculous	61
14.	Have Faith -Despite Your Circumstances	64
15.	Roots, Not Necessarily the Fruits	67
16.	True Conversion-Looks on No Man	69
17.	Prayer of Faith in The Right Place	71
18.	God Places His Burden in Me for Souls	75
19.	My First Message Preached	78
20.	God Given Vision for The Lost At All Cost	82
21.	Received Baptism-Speaking the Word of God with Boldness	87
22.	God's Continued Call for The Lost At All Cost	90
23.	Spiritual Boldness in Word and in Song	93
24.	Back to My Old Grounds-With New Grounds	95

#		
25.	Washington For Jesus a Must-Faith of Michael Abraham	97
26.	Glorying in My Flesh – God's Thorn	101
27.	Sensitivity to Our Fleshly Sins Brings Deliverance	104
28.	God Given Job – God Kept Job	109
29.	Heathen Co-workers – Become God's Workers	111
30.	Faith of a Little Child	114
31.	God's Favor in the Courts	116
32.	Debt Way Overdue – Paid in Full	119
33.	Prayer of Faith Astounds the Doctors and The Courts	122
34.	God Spoken – Thanksgiving Through Faith	124
35.	Faith Through Prayer – God's Supernatural Method	126
36.	God Given Faith to Reach Children	128
37.	Faith Tested – Outcome Miraculous	131
38.	Continuing to Be His Witness-Despite My Greatest Trial	134
39.	To Have Faith with No Faith in Sight	140
40.	Bahamas Gift Cruise – Given in Pure Love	143
41.	God's Miraculous Healing Power-Baby	146
42.	Testimony to My Supervisor – Gods Miraculous Healing Power	149
43.	God's Miraculous Multiplication	152
44.	Can We Do Like Jesus said – Turn the Other Cheek?	156
45.	Miraculous Love Brings Miraculous Deliverance	159
46.	Infatuation Can Take You Down the Wrong Path	163
47.	God's Deliverance from Rock and Roll Music	167
48.	Deliverance of Black Sabbath Worshippers	172
49.	The Power of Prayer with Faith	175
50.	God's Faith Assignment-Bible College	179

Faith Adventures Episode 1
God's Imprints in My Life Before Christ

God spared my life through His intervening work of grace – long before I knew He was calling me to ministry. I know this to be true due to specific instances that occurred even during the early years of my adolescence. My mother told me that I had contracted a severe case of strep throat shortly after I was born, which could have killed me, but with God's grace, I survived. As I was growing up, I became a normal, venturesome eight- year old boy. My childhood friend Tim and I loved to explore new places, disregarding the danger that may have lain ahead. In one instance, we were traveling to a very hazardous, marked-off area in the woods to play. Not heeding the warning signs, I carelessly slipped into some kind of quicksand pit. As I sank, I called to Tim and he quickly came to my rescue, pulling me out.

I remember at the age of ten going on a weekend camping trip with my family and another family, whose son by the name of John was a close friend of mine. Like most kids, we were very curious and ventured off away from the campsite. We happened to come across a Boy Scout troop whom we followed, doing whatever we saw them do. We knew it was wrong, but there was no fun in life unless you knew you were getting away with something. As we followed behind the troop, we approached a rushing stream. Hopping from one rock to another, we began to cross over. The rocks were very slippery, but everyone else successfully reached the other side. I was the last one in line, but my attempt to cross this stream failed. I fell right in while the others continued their course, unaware of my dilemma. As I went under, I gasped for breath in a panic. Once again, I could have brought about my own death, but somehow I was swept by the waters and rushed to a nearby embankment. I believe God with His accompanying angels shifted me to the shore. No one was there to rescue me. I have no other explanation other than the fact that God had rescued me.

I have done many other exciting feats, like jumping and hanging out of trees for dear life. I never had a broken bone in all my rebellious years of childhood, despite all of my crazy endeavors. The things you do in your younger years with no worries makes you think you are indestructible. This is all part of how boys were brought up in the exciting times of the 1950's. I believe this was also preparation for the days to come.

At the age of twenty, I landed a job working for a company that built car radios. I used to drive to work along with two other co-workers, Mary and Tony. One day, Tony who was usually with us had called in sick, so Mary and I went in to work by ourselves in my vehicle. It had rained heavily the night before, so the roads were coated with water making it very slippery. At the time, the tread on my tires was extremely low. Because of this, while driving, I lost control of the vehicle. The car turned around and around, sliding sideways into a utility pole. The driver-side door was completely torn off, thrusting me out of the car. I thought it was all over for me.

Miraculously, I was able to pick my body up and lean it against the car. As the paramedics arrived, they wrapped a headdress around my skull to stop the profuse bleeding from my head. Although it was split open and I had lost a lot of blood; I survived this near-fatal accident.

I remember feeling dizzy, but aware enough to be concerned about the vehicle. Out of selfishness, I cried to God, thinking only of myself and the first car I had ever purchased with every cent that I earned. It was a '61 Chevrolet Vista, blue, in excellent shape. To keep up with the times and the girls, I had my engine changed from a six cylinder to a 283 V8 to be more part of the groove.

I was a much-calloused man before I met Christ. I didn't even think of Mary other than how high my insurance was about to go up or how I might potentially get sued because of the accident. However, I was spared even though Mary's husband tried his best to sue, but was unsuccessful. You might say it was God's faithfulness towards me when I knew nothing about faith. According to Romans 5:8 AMP, "God showed and clearly proved His own love for us by the fact that while we were still sinners, Christ (the Messiah, the Anointed One) died for us."

Have you discovered through your journey with Him what a faithful God He really is? He is faithful in every way, each and every day? There will be trials that will come our way, though if we look at them rightly, they can prepare us for trials in the days to come. Do you understand that through everything that happens, God has a plan and a purpose for your life that He destined for you before the foundation of this world? If we really believe this, we can see God's imprints in our lives before Christ. I don't believe for a second that these happenings in my life were coincidences. I think if we would consider these things; we might see God at work in our lives outside of Christ. These were clearly God's incidences (His Interventions), designed to raise me up for this time.

When we're born, God can designate us for the purposed plan He has designed for our lives. I was born in 1947 for this time to be an instrument to the Jews as well as the Gentiles. According to

2 Peter 3:9 AMP, "The Lord does not delay and is not tardy or slow about what He promises, according to some people's conception of slowness, but He is longsuffering toward you, not desiring that any should perish, but that all should turn to repentance." This adventure, like every other adventure, should lead us to become more and more exciting, day after day, year after year, about what Christ can do in our lives if we are willing to truly follow Him, His ways, and His teachings. This can be the reality of His life working and His Spirit dwelling in us.

Faith Adventures Episode 2
The Blizzard That Blew Me Away

Growing up in Maryland, I remember experiencing a brisk winter when I was in the sixth grade. I will never forget Mrs. Blizzard, my teacher at the time. – Boy, when you approached her, she was like a blizzard! She taught me a lesson about truth that would forever change me. One day, during recess, the time I looked forward to the most during my schooldays, Mrs. Blizzard stalked toward me just as I was conversing in some unwholesome dialogue with my classmates. As I was speaking, she came up behind me. With her stout body, she grabbed me and spun me around to face her. I was in a state of total shock!

Without hesitation, she marched me to the principal's office. As a twelve- year old, this was the last place I wanted to be. Fear gripped me tighter than Mrs. Blizzard. I felt like my feet had been lifted off the ground. This was not an out of the body experience, but I sure would have welcomed one. To my dismay, when the principal's staff began to address this matter, they concluded that I cursed Mrs. Blizzard. I knew the truth, yet no one seemed to see it my way. She had me. I stood guilty. I even tried to defend myself over and over but to no avail. They were taking the teacher's side—not what I would have called fair play. I watched many television shows and the ones I watched led me to believe that everything would turn out okay. Unfortunately, I realized that from what I was experiencing, there were no easy answers within reach.

I felt frozen and trapped with no escape. They approached and cornered me in the office, saying with strong voices, "You must admit you cursed the teacher or else!" Standing bewildered, I replied in a soft tone, "Or else what?" "We will expel you for three days." My first thought was what was going to happen when I arrived home. My dad was never around too much anyway, but with my luck, would have been home for this occasion. With all my being, I didn't want to do what the staff was demanding, but what other choice did I have? I did what they asked and went back to class. To this day, I still don't think my parents ever knew. My relief grew with each day that passed after that knowing my parents never found out.

However, what happened haunted me. I didn't like what I had experienced and thought about this for a long time. The fact that I thought about anything was usually far from my experience. I truly believe God had somehow planned this episode to do something in me. It developed within me a spirit of honesty and truthfulness. I wouldn't allow anyone to put me in a spot like this again. I cannot explain this in any other way.

Maybe you have had something similar happen to you that shook your world. The problem is, too many of us don't recognize these things as God things. As I think back now; I probably only made this determination to suit my own purposes. After all, I knew no other way to live but the way I taught myself to get what I wanted out of life. John 4:24 tells us that God desires us to worship Him "in spirit and in truth." Maybe God gave me a sense of becoming a worshipper. Since the Lord changed my life, I determined in my heart to obey Him and no other. He spoke something to me later that I have never forgotten. He said, "My son – you are going to have to become the exact opposite of what you've been all your life." That was a pretty tall order! I responded and humbly said, "Lord, you are going to have to help me with all this." God has been faithful from the beginning, even until this day.

If He has ordained us from the foundation of the world to worship and serve Him, could He not in our early lives have done things we didn't understand at the time that would eventually bring us to a place where we could worship Him and Him alone? If God worked in our lives before we knew Him, can you imagine what He can do once we do know Him?

Faith Adventures Episode 3
Rationalization Catches You in Its Trap

Before I knew Christ; I began stealing little things and in time, went on to bigger crimes. This is where rationalization began to take its course. This was due to my carnal way of thinking. One day, my friend Tom and I, went into the Rexall Drug Store with pre-planned notions. That store today, would be about the size of a Family Dollar Store with many varieties of items to choose from. We stole everything in sight to our delight. We disregarded a large warning sign about what would happen to shoplifters. Later, consequences followed. The sign offered a reward of fifty dollars for information leading to the apprehension of shoplifters.

Up to this time in my earlier years, I worked for everything. This seemed at the time the easy way of getting anything we wanted without working for it. I was never taught any differently. We made a grave mistake by bragging to our friend about how we got away with our crime. This so-called friend reported us to the authorities, but I don't think he got the fifty dollars.

In those days they would send someone out to bring us to justice. First the authorities went to Tom's home, and his father, Mr. Starnes, a fairly husky man, brought the authorities to my front door. My father, a rather tall and slim man answered the door and told the authorities I wasn't home. I was in our back yard around the corner of our house, listening. I saw them at the door and I could hardly keep myself from bursting out, while hearing everything they were saying.

I didn't know the Scriptures then, but I was about to discover one I couldn't escape.

Numbers 22:23 states, "You can be sure your sins will find you out." In another one of my escapades soon after that, my dad had found a package of pens he knew I had stolen. When he asked me about them, I was shaking in my boots and frightfully responded with the wrong answer. He took me back to marketplace store to face the manager and admit I had stolen these items. At that time, I remembered, my dad had told me if I went to jail, that I was there to stay. My dad had never shown any compassion and this day wasn't any different. I could see the compassion in the female manager's countenance, because we brought the items back. I was relieved because I could have been sitting behind bars.

This spirit of insensitivity which I probably inherited from my father followed me into my later years. I was riding on the back of my friend Tom's motorcycle and we were traveling rather slowly. I said something to my friend that was soon to bring me pain and discomfort. " Give it some gas, brother. " Suddenly, we went up into the air and I toppled off the back, only to bounce quite a few times on the pavement. My light jacket was torn to shreds and my back was in excruciating pain. I didn't bother to go to a doctor. Instead, I went home to smoke some marijuana to relieve my pain. If it wouldn't have been for my Christian neighbor Bill persisting to take me to see a doctor, I probably wouldn't have gone.

My point in this is to demonstrate a spirit of insensitivity which was probably inherited from my dad. This spirit caused me to not even care about my own body. This kind of blindness could no doubt, cause you to not have compassion for those even the closest to you. This will be further shared in future Faith Adventures; how this affected me in compassion for others in ministry.

God has impressed on me that I thought I was getting away with a lot of things in life. The truth that later bothered me is that it was to the misfortune of others. This fleshly spirit of insensitivity to someone else's dilemma has followed me down through the years. On several occasions, others have helped me in my dilemmas. With all my being I tried to keep from bursting out at theirs. Sometimes on the job I would be talking to a client seriously about a matter and this flesh, unaware, would rise up only to find out later it actually happened. This has carried on with me for many years ——to this day ——and has gotten me in a whole lot of trouble. We can be so misunderstood because of how our flesh reacts before Christ and after God has truly changed us. As a believer, we are not accountable for something we are unaware of within our human make up. James 4:17 AMP states, "So any person who knows what is right to do but does not do it, to him it is sin."

The Holy Spirit which lives in us can and will direct us to make things right. When we respond with a broken and contrite spirit in true repentance to God and others in our failures; that's all we can continue to do, to be pleasing to God. We may have to face the consequences in this life, but more importantly in the next life——in God's judgment of all mankind —— we are forgiven! Thanks, be to God, He forgives us of all our sins and shortcomings. According to Isaiah 64:8, He is the Potter and we are the clay. He is making and molding us each and every day! God's still working on me in what He wants me to be. How about you? Is He still working on you also?

Faith Adventures Episode 4
False Seed of Religion Keeps Us from Real Relationship

I strongly believe there is a seed in the church (the Body of Christ) that appears to be God's seed, but really is not. Messiah Jesus illustrated this in the parable of the wheat and tares. According to Matthew 13:25, the enemy had sowed tares among the wheat. These tares are referred to as darnel wheat. They were not good for much of anything, like weeds.

Darnel wheat appears to be genuine wheat, but is not. A species of rye-grass has seeds of which consist of a deadly poison. The symptoms are sleepiness, drowsiness, convulsions, drunkenness, trembling, inability to walk, hindered speech, vomiting, and dim-sightedness.

This describes the physical symptoms, but we can plainly see in the church many of these spiritual symptoms. Many of us are not attentive as we should be and in some cases, fall asleep during the message. Watchfulness is something we rarely see to stay on top of things, the best that we can be. Most of us are devoid when it comes to having spiritual insight. Too many of us have our mind on earthly things which could cause us brain disorders, when God said we need to set our minds on the things above. We are often bold in the excitement of earthly entertainment like drunkenness, and lack the same excitement in the Godly matters. We are self-driven and our speech never seems to change. We tremble when life's blows hit us the hardest, but the majority of us never change. His Word gives us the ability to walk and mature, but we choose to hear, but not obey. Let's be honest with ourselves. We know by God's strength alone we can be what God has designed us to be. This defines so many of us in our churches today!

I believe God's seed can be soiled with so much religion, that a person on the outside can't see the tree of life in the whole forest. Mark 4:11-12 illustrates this beautifully. Jesus was saying to them, 'To you has been given the mystery of the kingdom of God, but those who are outside get everything in parables, so that WHILE SEEING, THEY MAY SEE AND NOT PERCEIVE, AND WHILE HEARING, THEY MAY HEAR AND NOT UNDERSTAND, OTHERWISE THEY MIGHT RETURN AND BE FORGIVEN." Religion can double-blind us to reality, masking (veiling) both the glory of the living LORD as well as the ugliness of our failures.

As a young boy, I occasionally attended this big Baptist church that sat on the top of the hill for all to see. I remember Jim, my Sunday school teacher that took time to talk to me. He spoke into my soul, outside the four walls of the church. He was the only one that reached out to me. Jim was a tall, thin, man with curly black hair and he was the Sunday school teacher. He had been delivered from alcohol and he would tell his testimony often. My dad was also an alcoholic, but I never saw any change in him until he later met death's door. I barely remember this church and even less the people that attended. I do remember my neighbor Christian friends. These twin boys, Billy and Bobby Shockley, acted like they were serious and took hold of my arms and literally dragged me to an altar of prayer!

I went along reluctantly and prayed the sinner's prayer. I know to this day I sincerely didn't mean it from my heart. Only God knew the truth of this matter. I determined in my heart not to get baptized, which was their next step. Quickly, I went to the men's room for a break from all this, avoiding baptism like the plaque. These same two boys lived across the street from me in our housing development called Maple Crest in Baltimore County, Maryland. One day, they meant harm to me by both of them jumping me and beating on me until I bit one of them and the other one took off running to his home. They professed to know Him, like many of us, but fell short of living it like the majority.

I will never forget what happened in this same church one Sunday morning in my later years after graduating from Overlea Senior High School. I was gladly attending to be with my childhood sweetheart, Susan. She was seventeen, the girl of my dreams out of all the other girls that I had dated. I stopped dating them all because I surely thought she was the one. The leaders were all dressed up in the old type tweed suits. They stepped up to the podium proudly in the front of the whole congregation and approached the pulpit and had the audacity to read off name by name those that had not given their tithes. I took notice they didn't read off their own names. Romans 3:23, "We all fall short of God's Glory!" I told my girlfriend, "I don't know much about what is going on in this place, but I know what they are doing is not right and I will see you later." I got so angry, I stomped out of the church and I don't think I entered their doors again. I was a product of looking upon man's epitome of pride in its highest dimension. Pride blocks us all from God, but with humility we can all draw near to Him.

It's one thing for us to look on man outside of Christ, but to look on man knowing Christ is a whole other thing. God warned us of making men or women idols in the Book of Deuteronomy. Sad to say, many of us look on man to this day. We should only look on man if he truly is an imitator of Christ in word and deed and truly walking in obedience to Christ.

Satan had put on my mind for the longest time a false picture of true Christianity.

For many years, my thoughts were as follows: these Christians are not having any fun and they're not excited about what they have, so why do I want this? I'm living an exciting life in sin and enjoyed it to its fullest! My thoughts were also that, maybe I will think about this when I'm sixty- five or when I get married. If I'm going to be miserable, I would like to have someone to share my misery with me.

The soiled seed is in far too many of our churches today. It has been my own personal experience to show compassion in asking any believer this question: are you where we all need to be in partaking of His Word on a daily basis? I would say from my experience that 90% of the believers or more haven't received God's real seed. Many believers new in the Lord have not been made disciples, nor has someone become their friend to help guide them. I had a pastor disciple me for a short time, and then I listened to a bible-based pastor on television to receive discipleship training. I'm not judging believers, but the system they have allowed themselves to be under many times is unbiblical and unpleasing to God. Isn't it amazing that according to Matthew 28:18-19, this is the one thing that Jesus Christ told us to do, make disciples, and this is overlooked to be the least the church does even to this day...

Faith Adventures Episode 5
Relationships in the Flesh can be Deceiving

There is something all of us want in our lives. That is, a real relationship, if we knew it could be possible. I'm not talking about something that is perfect in every way. If we think of relationships in this way we really don't understand God's whole plan. The world has painted us a picture that is a fantasy and this has influenced our minds through music, movies, television, the general media and other person's opinions. Music was my escape from reality and convinced me that a relationship with a woman was the greatest thing that could happen to me.

The Lord told us to beware of the philosophies of this world (Colossians 2:8) because He knew they have trapped us into its way of thinking, which is the complete opposite of God's Word and what He says about life. It has taken all of our lives to become what we are. How could we possibly expect Him to change us overnight?

When I was growing up in Baltimore, I saw what others had, and wanted this also.

Because I was shy, my personality kept me from a lot of relationships that probably wouldn't have been good for me anyway. I was so shy I couldn't get up enough courage to ask someone to my senior prom. I wanted a relationship more than anything else because I had waited so long.

I not only wanted a relationship, but I wanted a beautiful girl. This made me very choosy and that was probably a good thing also to keep me out of a lot of bad relationships. God was doing this very thing, but I never realized this until now. He was keeping me from living out the ultimate self-gratification of my fleshly desires. He was keeping me from death's door, so to speak.

I really liked to go bowling and there I met my child sweetheart, Susan. She gave me her home telephone number the very first night and I was really soaring! She was seventeen and everything I dreamed of in having a steady girlfriend. I was twenty and out of school and I was more than willing to wait for her. I knew from the start she was the only girl for me. I never looked at another girl and was faithful to her throughout all of our years of our relationship. I called her every night for over two years and showed her off to everyone. She was faithful through and through.

There were many nights I went out with close friends who were many times unfaithful to their wives. I couldn't understand how my friend could do this to their good wives. I don't know why, but Belair Road was the place to be. I hung out there practically every night, it was another one of my escapes from my dysfunctional family. This particular night we were driving around, and we came across two girls in distress with a flat tire and we fixed it for them. They invited us into a restaurant to have a bite to eat to get to know us better. I was going along with this for my friend's sake, although Marvin was married to one of the most wonderful women that ever walked on this earth. And then it happened, something I never expected!

Laurie said she remembered me from school and had tried to get my attention many times. I was shy in my high school years and never responded to any girl. She kept pursuing me, saying how she wished that it could've been different. My relationship with Susan at that time wasn't as good as I would have liked it to be. I wanted more out of it, and she was trying to control me. I was having a hard-enough time in my life controlling my flesh. At this time Susan was extremely upset with me over a menial matter. Laurie and I went to her place and she fulfilled my desires for about a month and I knew I had become unfaithful to my girlfriend. I enjoyed these times with Laurie, but I realized this was not true love.

Something within me kept telling me to tell my sweetheart about this and ask her forgiveness. Most every one of my friends advised me not to tell her. The reason I told her was because of this work many years before that God had done within me about truth and honesty. She was a Christian and occasionally I went to church with her. Naturally, I thought that she would forgive me. I was in for the shock of my life, because she not only wouldn't forgive me, but she left me.

After this happened, I didn't care who I was with to get what I wanted. I was still honest with every one of them. I would never lie to get what I wanted out of a relationship. Most of us men put up our walls to keep from getting hurt again and again. This caused me to mistreat many women and I'm ashamed of that to this day. When I think of them today I pray for them. After years of very short relationships, I got tired of this fleshly life and I wanted a relationship. There were a few that had never worked out, but I had learned my lesson and was never unfaithful again.

Soon after, I met my beauty queen Darlene in a bar and fell in love with her because she was attractive to me. I stuck with her, even though she was unfaithful with my best friend. This happened just before we were leaving Maryland to come to Florida. I was married to her for six years (you will read more about this in other Faith Adventures) and I was faithful for all those years.

Although she left me a couple times, I still remained faithful to her. When Christ changed my life, it became more that I was faithful to God, by being faithful to my wife. This was the real relationship I needed, not knowing anything about a relationship with God our Creator.

If we have sinned against others, we don't have the revelation that David had (Psalms 51) and that is ultimately, we have sinned against God our Creator. If we will truly humble ourselves, we will realize He knows more about life than anyone. When He has truly changed us, we will no longer listen to these philosophies.

Eleven years later, God brought Nubia, the one He specially picked for me and we have been married now for twenty-five years now with two teens. I have been completely faithful to God and my wife. God willing, you will read about this in the Faith Adventures to come.

Faith Adventures Episode 6
Joey Clarke: My Nephew's Story – Gone into Glory

"When I was in my twenties, I was as wild as I could be
I was therefore never home or around for my family to see
As time went by, my sister Carol – next oldest to me
Got married, but not until later did it became news to me
I met her husband of the Hindu faith named Randy
Also, her son Joey – who at that time was the age of three
Joey – however, wasn't Randy's birth child and began being abused physically
Due to rage that settled within Randy – acceptance of Joey became his inability."

My eldest sister Carol was enduring a very troubled and dysfunctional marriage. Because the situation between her and her husband was becoming more severe, she was about to make a hasty decision. Out of desperation, my sister considered putting her son Joey up for adoption. When she told me this, I felt compassion for my nephew and desired for him to have a good home. Aside from my biological mother, there was a woman by the name of Pat who, over time, became like a second mother to me. Not knowing what to do, I contacted her for advice unaware that down the line, she would arrange for her sister to adopt my nephew Joey.

This was another one of God's supernatural workings, though I had no clue at that moment.

One day I received an unexpected call from Joey, who was by then fourteen. He couldn't thank me enough for the part God had me play in his life. I was thrilled by the thought of how God used me, considering that I didn't care much for anyone but myself. I told him how

Christ had changed my life. It was quite a while before I had heard from Joey again. In fact, the next time I did was when he was in his twenties. He told me that he had received Jesus as his personal Lord and Savior. I prayed for and encouraged him – giving God all the glory for a prayer of mine that had been answered. Unfortunately, it wasn't long after Joey received Christ that I received a distressing call from my sister Carol. Once again, my God-given faith was tested. Joey, like so many others, battled deep rooted issues and began using drugs. Many people have been dragged down by substance abuse like alcohol, drugs and even sex. My nephew was no exception – allowing the struggles of life to gnaw on him continually. I served as a chaplain for three years with a ministry of recovering alcoholics and drug addicts. I knew from experience what Joey's problem was, and like so many I worked with, he wouldn't deal with it.

Joey had only served God for a very short time and his life was like a revolving door. During his spiritual walk with the Lord, he became part of programs and missions. I would always tend to hear from him when things seemed to be going well. However, when things were rough, I didn't hear from him at all and would be prompted by God's Spirit to call and check in on him. At one particular moment in Joey's life, he was involved with a woman whom I knew was not in God's will for him regarding a soul mate. Something more disturbing at that time came out of my nephew's mouth. He couldn't come to forgiveness towards his mother for giving him away. I tried to explain that what my sister did was for his protection, but he didn't understand and went on venting about it.

God used me again to minister to him by explaining that, like any one of us, he could only forgive his mother through the strength that can only come from God. Still, he failed to hear what I was trying to express regarding his mother's decision. My church even prayed for his deliverance from unforgiveness when my nephew happened to visit one day. I've realized that when bitterness and unforgiveness are working, people speak as though there is no real problem and manage to say things like, "Well, God knows my heart." That is how you know someone has deceived themselves—they speak these things, but know nothing.

Sadly enough, about a year later – I received a shocking phone call. Joey was dead at age forty-two. I heard that in the last three months before his passing, he was fervently seeking the Lord, going to a Baptist church and attending Bible studies. I believe though that because he was not dealing with his issue of forgiveness, the enemy drew him back to taking drugs again. This time, he had gotten hold of a very lethal drug which ultimately brought him to his end. He was found frozen to death at the front entrance of the very same church where he was prayed for regarding his "forgiveness." I believe Joey knew he was dying – so he reached out to God and according to the Lord's merciful hand, my nephew's prayer was answered.

By faith, I believe, and have claimed my nephew's soul for the Kingdom of God. I would also say this to you and believe our Father in Heaven would say the same thing in a much greater volume: Don't let bitterness, anger, or unforgiveness get into your heart. Don't even let it get its start! These ungodly manifestations have been slaying many men and women out of their place in Christ. Many men and women of the world and professing believers have gone down this path far too many times. I have come to this conclusion from my own personal experiences ministering to others. Our problem is that we haven't dealt with the hard blows in our lives. If we don't deal with these deep-rooted issues, they can take us down a path that we thought we would never be on. Let Joey's story be an encouragement to you to pray and have the eyes of faith for others when they don't have this for themselves! God through His Son, Jesus Christ never gave up on us, so how can we give up on others?

Faith Adventures Episode 7
Mom's Faithful Prayers

Now this Faith Adventure is about what happens when you have someone faithfully praying for you. Although I had a maternal mother, the Lord graced me with a beautiful woman of God who became like a second mother to me. Her name was Pat, a fairly short woman with rosy cheeks – sweeter than anyone I ever knew. This woman prayed for me for over fifty years and you knew that when she said she loved you, you could see in her face that she meant it.

My mother – Pat, was continually on her knees day and night praying for her children. She never excluded anyone, including me, that God would bring her way and was known for rescuing children or anyone off the street with no fear for her own safety.

I met Pat and her husband Mel when I was very young. Mel was a red headed, thin man that loved to drink tea and smoke Raleigh cigarettes by the pack daily. He managed a coin collector shop where I began my first coin collection. They had three children; two boys, Jay and George, and one girl, Rue Anne – all younger than me. They were considered my family when I was away from home. Every time I would visit them, I felt and could sense the love in this family.

Out of all my numerous life stories, there are two that are so incredibly unbelievable to me. I'm going to share what happened due to the prayers of my mother. I believe God was intervening for me on behalf of her and her level of fervency.

Contrary to being a hard-conscientious worker, I was an extreme partier who loved women, nightclubs, rock music and everything that goes along with it. At the age of twenty, someone turned me on to marijuana. I liked it a lot; especially since it didn't have an effect on my body like alcohol did considering that I was into bodybuilding at the time. For many years, I continued using marijuana that eventually led to other drugs. Though these other drugs were mostly ones I experimented on, they took me places I didn't want to be. I was more content with smoking marijuana to remain in a place or state that I thought was reality.

Some of my friends, however, became addicted to the other drugs. Believe it or not, I had such a concern for my friends that I intentionally took some type of mind altering drug to see if I could experience what was happening with them. The drug took me completely out of reality and I found myself reliving a Rock n' Roll song by Alice Cooper about how he couldn't find his way back home. I didn't like the feeling of being away from reality. Unexplainably, I was beginning to experience something that caused me to beg my friends to get off this drug. This had to have been God's compassion coming out of me. Again, He works in mysterious ways. Fortunately, I received news shortly after that my friends had ceased consuming the drugs on an weekly basis. Before I had even come to Christ, God had actually given me a poem that seemed to just come right out of the sky! I actually shared it with many of my friends, not understanding what God was saying – but it was full of his truth.

> "Life is not what it seems to be
> Although people don't live in reality
> People are always reaching out for something there
> The only trouble is that they're unaware.
> If games were meant for people to play
> There wouldn't be such a thing as the Sabbath day
> We all should learn to love one another
> We all should live like sister and brother.

I have only this to say
I wish people would be more honest with each other today."

At this point in my life, I loved marijuana so much that I began selling it. This was not even to get rich but just to have extra money to go on some really cool vacations. One night, I was at a club called the Latin Casino. Stephen, a friend of mine at the time asked me to go out to my car. I should have known better than to go knowing he didn't really carry that great of a reputation. He began telling me about some marijuana that I had never heard of or tried. We eventually got in my car and ended up lighting one up. During that, someone happened to open up the passenger door and asked my friend Stephen for some cigarette papers – probably smelling the marijuana. There was no reason to be paranoid because this went on quite frequently.

Then – all of a sudden, my door flung wide open. The man shouted, "State Police – hold everything you got!" I immediately put out the marijuana and I was attempting to swallow the remaining evidence. He pulled me out of my car, put me up against it and began spreading my legs. I don't remember him reading me my rights. In my attempt to swallow the marijuana, I was choking for a short time before it finally went down into my system. I turned around like I was innocent and said to the officer," Now what's the problem?", defiantly telling him that it was a cigarette to make a fool out of him. The officers then decided to thoroughly search my car, unable to find anything. That was something for me considering all the times that I had broken the law.

They did happen to open the trunk, finding something they didn't recognize. It was a new Rainbow vacuum cleaner that I was trying to sell. I said to them when they pulled it out of my trunk," Would you like a demonstration?" Knowing that they had no evidence against me, I played them like fools and was totally disrespectful. They then decided that they would take Stephen and me downtown to the Police headquarters. Along the way, my friend was trying to put all the blame on me to save his own skin. As they checked my records though, they couldn't find any felonies or misdemeanors. After checking Stephen's records, they discovered he was wanted for a felony so they took him into the Police Station and locked him up. The officers decided that they would take me back to my car. When we got there, they asked me if I was going back into the nightclub. I told them probably not because of this experience. They then had the audacity to ask me for my tickets which I had already purchased. I told them "yes" and soon afterwards tore them up and threw them into their faces knowing they had nothing on me. Therefore, what did I have to lose?

About a week later, I had just picked up a new pound of marijuana to take it across town to sell. Something was about to happen that I would have never expected. When I stopped at a red light – there was those same two officers from the nightclub parking lot squad. At this point, I had no doubt if seen, what the outcome would have been. Fearful thoughts began racing through my mind like, "If they saw me, they would arrest me and throw away the key!" Now this was God working on my behalf because a good friend of mine was arrested and sentenced to five years for just a quarter of a pound of marijuana. In those days, when the police arrested you for a drug charge – you went into the slammer.

There was one other time that I recall was a very close call. I just had purchased a pound on another night and was only a couple blocks from home. An old girlfriend was following me home from the pick-up. All of a sudden, we were both being pulled over by a county policeman. I was high at the time, but I could still think fast. I had just remembered getting a warning for an inspection for my car. Without hesitation, I quickly reached into my glove compartment and retrieved the inspection citation – already getting the matter taken care of. I immediately got out of my car because the pound of marijuana was in my front seat! I approached the officer and said to him that I knew why he had stopped me and showed him the inspection citation that was taken care of. Getting sidetracked having a conversation with my then girlfriend, he ended up relieving me and said I could go. I swiftly got into my car and drove just around the corner to my home. I quickly pulled up at my home and locked my car with the marijuana in the front seat. I dashed into my place and was looking out for him to come around the corner any minute. Paranoia gripped me and it seemed like it was hours. Thoughts were racing through my mind that maybe my girlfriend had spilled the beans and they were coming to arrest me. Finally, my girlfriend came to my home, but the officer never came down our street. I never thought these things were happening in this manner because of my mother's prayers for me and the fact that God had a plan for my life.

Do you have someone like this in your life? A praying mother or father? I want to encourage any of you that are reading this account that when we pray for others that we know are sinners and living it to their fullest to never give up on them. Someone said that Jesus' Prayers were the shortest, but had the longest reach. Let's pray when the Holy Spirit prompts us to pray and have faith that God will steer them His Way. Never give up on those that God brings your way.

Faith Adventures Episode 8
God's Calling Could Be Unknown

One summer as a young boy, I was working a job helping customers coming out of the supermarkets take groceries to their car. It wasn't a regular job, but I received tips for my labor. That day, a gentleman by the name of Joe stopped to speak to me. He was the bread vendor who delivered to the local neighborhood stores. A gray-headed man in his early forties, he drove a step van displaying the huge bread advertisement, "Schmidt's Blue Ribbon Bread" in yellow and blue and wore the uniform to match. He asked me, "Would you like to ride around with me so I can teach you the business?" "I would like to," I replied. He didn't pay me, but I figured I would go for it since my only form of work was helping customers load their groceries into their cars. I really enjoyed riding around with Joe – learning and meeting people. He would always give me bread and snacks to take home.

At the age of twenty-five, I had just experienced a major layoff from a job doing some carpentry-construction work. This period of time lasted for three months. I could barely pay my rent and had very little to eat. I was living on mayonnaise sandwiches practically every day. One day, I was walking in my neighborhood and saw Joe, the old bread vendor. After all these years, I managed to cross paths with him while he was making a delivery on the same route he had done years ago when we first met. I approached Joe and asked if there was a possibility I could get hired. Joe promised to speak to his supervisor and give me a good recommendation. He did mention something that could have made it more difficult for me to get a job there. The company since its inception only hired within their own families. Still, I went in for the interview all clean shaved and the supervisor seemed to like me. However, there wasn't anything available at the time. I did ask if it would be alright for me to call from time to time to check on any potential openings and I was assured that it was fine.

I made it a point to call every other month. About a year later, I was informed about a route opening up downtown where I lived. The thought of working in Baltimore City frightened me because of the crime I noticed on the nightly news. I ended up accepting the job. In my period of waiting, I allowed my facial hair to grow out. The supervisor Steve approached me and noticed that I had grown a little more hair since the last time he met me. He said, "What do you intend to do about this matter?" In a prideful manner, I told him that I would consider it and trim it up to make myself look more presentable. I don't think he liked my response to his question by the appearance of his distasteful countenance.

I heard shortly after this that the matter was reported to the Vice President of the company whom I was called to meet with privately along with Steve, my supervisor. The Vice President asked Steve what area of town was I working in and Steve told him. To this day, the response from the Vice President still baffles me. He actually said, "If he is going to be among animals, then I guess it's ok if he looks like one!" Again, God works in mysterious ways! Over time, I decided to grow a beard and long hair. It was the early seventies and a very well-known movie was just released entitled, "Jesus Christ Superstar" that I went to see seven times. The whole plant heard about this and began calling me "Jesus Christ, Superstar."

Then–as well as today–I can honestly say that if God puts you in a place, you will be there until He says you are to leave. There was one time on the job; I was wrongly accused of stealing by a store manager. I believe that because God made me a good, conscientious worker–especially towards my customers; I never in any way shape or form cheated my customers with this kind of disrespect. I never took anything that wasn't mine. One of the sons of an employee would even brag to me and probably others that he would steal from his customers because they trusted him. I told him that if he continued doing this, he would surely lose his job. The son's father worked for the company a very long time and it came as a total shock to him what his son was doing when he eventually found out.

I was very thankful for my job, unaware that God had orchestrated the whole matter. There were many times when I would make a mistake like forgetting to give the customer all of their merchandise they paid for and I would still go back out of my way to give them their products. They trusted us as their vendors and often times never even checked to see what they purchased. This was something God had done in me in my earliest Faith Adventure experience with Mrs. Blizzard. The news of my level of honesty had even reached up to my supervisor.

On one other occasion, I was on my regular routine when he saw; I was wrongly accused of collecting money twice from a customer. My immediate supervisor at the time–Jim heard of this matter and stood by me regardless of what was stated. God had done a work in my life concerning my conscience to make me a man of integrity and I believe saw that. This was one of the worst days in my life–I had worked so hard to make good. I was experiencing being accused of something that I knew I hadn't done. I figure now that God may have allowed this incident to happen as a test to see how I would hold up in the future Faith Adventures to come. Soon after this, the store manager realized it was their mistake and apologized. I was so relieved when I heard this good news. I didn't know much about God back then–much less about giving Him thanks or giving Him Glory. I give God all the Glory today for what He had done then, now and the days which are yet to come!

I believe God was bringing me to a place where I would be more prepared for the future. People were kind and compassionate in the fifties. The Lord knew I needed that. If we were to put these people today in our world with that same mindset, it could potentially change our world for the better. Could God possibly put us in certain eras and arenas to make our calling and election sure?

Faith Adventures Episode 9
God's Deliverance from Being Prejudiced

What do we think of when we hear the word, "Prejudice?" We automatically assume what has happened between the white man and the black man. There are other prejudices, but this is at the top of the list. Could it possibly be this has been ingrained within us? My own experience and my upbringing revealed to me how this ungodly attitude can naturally develop within us.

My father was a tall, medium build man with curly hair who worked in Baltimore, Maryland at American Standard. He had a very hard job making bathroom fixtures with enamel in extremely hot conditions. Black men made up the majority of the population in Baltimore City, so of course, many of his co-workers were black. We lived on the outskirts, not too far from the city. When I was a little boy, I recall my father talking about how he would have encounters with his "black" co-workers and that many of them carried knives. After hearing this, I was traumatized by even the thought of what would happen if I were to meet a black man. I was somewhat relieved though when my family and I moved to Baltimore County. There were only a few young black men who went to my Junior High School. There was something that happened in my school though that may have placed me toward the path of deliverance.

There were two gangs at my school, but one in particular was prejudiced towards blacks. One day, they happened to beat up one young black student very badly and I heard that the other gang went up against them because of this incident. For that to happen was very rare. Back in that era, it was highly unlikely for a white man to fight against his own white brothers to defend a black man.

I'd like to take you back to the time when I received my first real job at the bakery that I mentioned in the last Faith Adventure. At this point, I had been training for a week and now I was ready to start my new route all on my own. I was given small business accounts and some supermarket accounts with my job. The bigger stores were a bit challenging for me at first concerning my issue. While I was in my truck, I remember not wanting to even get out on many occasions due to the fear that constantly raced through me. I never told anyone about this, but I eventually had to deal with the issue of being prejudiced throughout my life before Christ changed me. I never thought about it much back then, but somehow it dawned on me and I began realizing that this group of people were just like every other group of people. God was beginning my process of deliverance that I didn't understand until now as He was imprinting my life for today.

The Bible says in the Psalms 34:9 (NIV) that, "Fear the Lord you his holy people for those that fear Him lack nothing." That scripture was beginning to manifest in my life when I began training to be a bodybuilder. I trained so hard and was determined to get in shape, not only to develop a good physique, but to feel good. I also figured that because of my physique, I would be kept from all harm. Whatever the case was, I knew that I liked it and at the same time, God removed the fear almost completely out of my heart! One day while in route for my job, an incident occurred after all this deliverance of fear took place. Two young men came into my truck, took a loaf of bread and threw it on the ground daring me to pick it up and saying that if I did, they would knock my block off. I responded with no fear – looking them in the eyes and telling them to go ahead and try. They never did and it so happens that the altercation got all over the city that I was not afraid of anything or anyone!

Another one of my co-workers was scared to death every day. I tried telling him that if you show anyone trying to challenge you that you have no fear, then they will stop harassing you. If this mere experience of no fear occurred back then and had this kind of effect, how much greater should our lives affect others with the true fear of God on a daily basis?

We have all heard the expression that God works in mysterious ways on our behalf for our well-being and that His protection is mightily upon us by the presence of His Holy angels! If this kind of thing happened in my earlier years without Christ, how much more should this be happening today as a child of the Living God! You will read in the coming Faith Adventures how this can be.

Faith Adventures Episode 10
Beginning of Faith Impartation–Unbelievable

The first vacation I ever took was when I visited Florida after purchasing some real estate there. My biological mother was diagnosed with breast cancer and didn't have that much longer to live. It was always her dream to come to Florida so I figured I would take this opportunity to grant her that wish. God's creation intrigued me, especially the way the clouds moved down there. I fell in love with the state so much that I decided to relocate there and brought along with me my wife at the time, Darlene, and my brother Kevin. God motivated me to bring my brother because after my initial trip to Florida, my mother had finally passed away and I made a promise to her that I would take care of my brother. I knew God was at work in my life because I was able to land a job in Florida within a short time frame which enabled me to make the move there.

During the move to Florida, we rented a twenty-four foot U-Haul truck and traveled many tireless miles to reach our destination. While I drove the truck, Darlene followed behind me and it happened to be raining pretty bad on the way. As we entered the Georgia line that crosses into Florida–suddenly, Darlene's windshield wipers just stopped working. I made a hasty decision to pull over on the side of the road. The only problem was that there wasn't any pavement. I began trying to drive the U-Haul up a slight hill that turned into some type of mudslide. I attempted to pull up it many times out of prideful ambition, but began noticing that the U-Haul was about to turn over. When I realized my dilemma, it humbled me because I knew if I were to continue any more, I would have lost everything I owned. After an hour of being stuck, a man who noticed us pulled over to help. He told us he was going to get us a man with a small tow truck to attempt to get us out. We had no choice but to wait to see the outcome.

As he was attempting to pull me out, I could hear gears grinding while sitting on the edge of my seat. I couldn't believe that the man was actually able to pull the vehicle, and with ease. I was afraid to ask him how much it was going to cost me. When he told me that it only came out to $15.00, I could hardly believe what I was hearing. I quickly gave him $20.00 in hopes that there wasn't some kind of mistake. I didn't stay around to find out differently. It may have been that God put him in our path for that very purpose.

After arriving in Apalachicola, we had a deadline after unloading the truck to return it to Jacksonville as instructed to us by the manager where we initially picked it up. Darlene and I decided that on our way to return the U-Haul, we would get married at the Justice of the Peace. I hardly remember this occasion to this day because it happened so fast. We had no money or anything to eat, but a loaf of wheat bread. Most of our money was spent gassing up both the truck and the car to go on our 300-mile trip to Jacksonville. We ended up arriving too late to drop off the truck due to the bad weather – not to mention we had faulty windshield wipers. The rain was pouring down which made our trip much more hazardous. Since we were late, we had to wait for the entire night in an empty 24-foot U-Haul, which happened to be our honeymoon, for the place to open the next day. Of course, this affected Darlene and she was sorely disappointed. I tried to encourage her and let her know that a wonderful day was ahead of us in order to celebrate our honeymoon.

Finally, the people of the establishment showed up. As the manager was reviewing the rates, to my surprise–he told us that we owed him money and was even talking about taking the tires off of our car. I explained to him that I simply followed the instructions of the management whom I initially ordered the truck from in Maryland. So here we are–over 300 miles from home with a dollar and a loaf of bread, stuck in Jacksonville, Florida! Darlene had an idea to sell her new hair dryer to one of the seven pawn shops in the area. We went to all six without any luck. It wasn't until we entered the last one that the man wanted to buy her $32.00 hairdryer for just $3.00 for his daughter. At this point, our dilemma was not as bad–nonetheless, it was still disastrous.

I told Darlene to find the nearest gas station and put the $3.00 in the car. She questioned if that would be enough. I knew it wouldn't be, even as low as gas was back then, but I didn't want her to be concerned considering how worrisome she could be. I told her that we were just going to put the gas in and see how far it would take us. I cannot remember doing such a thing like this in my entire life. There was no doubt a measure of faith was coming out of me from God. I began to put the gas in and I took notice that I had 6 quarts of oil. I got excited and told Darlene that I would sell the oil at $0.25 a quart. I must have been crazy thinking I could sell oil at a gas station, but at that time in my life not knowing Christ; I was too prideful to ask anyone for anything. It wasn't long before a man approached me to purchase my oil. He told me that normally he wouldn't do that but he had just quit his job. This was another God-incidence I believe that was happening back then.

If I was that crazy in all the things I did for myself and probably pleasing our adversary, how much more should I be crazy for the One Who gave His all for you and me! Many today probably think I'm crazy and that's okay by me. At least I'm crazy for my Lord. Now–finally–my life has reason. I was shy at one point, but since knowing Christ, coming out of my shell has allowed me to arise for Our Lord.

You will read about the miraculous change God made in my life in the next Faith Adventure!

Faith Adventures Episode 11
Life in Christ After Being Born Again!

Carrabelle was a small, country town in Florida with a population of about 1,500 people. Because it was so small, if you drove through the area – a blink of the eye and you could miss it. The police station was nothing but a telephone booth and was actually featured on a television show called "You Asked For It." At the time, this is where God stationed me to be.

The city of Carrabelle joined with Apalachicola in order to serve Apalachicola as a bread vendor for all their stores. Because of this, I was able to make a decent living selling and delivering bread while building a business for the company I was working for called Flowers Baking Company.

During this time, my wife Darlene and I were experiencing marital issues at home even though we paid a few visits to a local church. One day, she claimed to have given her life to the Lord yet was throwing pots and pans at me that very night. Leaving her presence was the only way I knew how to deal with life's blows. Unfortunately, a year later – she decided to leave me. This was something that I had never experienced before. She was the woman of my dreams – not to mention, very beautiful. After investing all that I had into this great relationship, I thought that this time it would be different compared to all of the ones before. I thought this was what I wanted, that this was the answer – but I came to the realization that a relationship with a woman was not the real answer.

Work wasn't going very well either. I had a new supervisor by the name of Ray who was a real test for me at this time in my life. He was a short, pudgy man that moved on his feet rather slowly. He decided one day to ride with me during my route to evaluate my work ethics. Not only was he telling me what to do, but he would poke his finger into my chest in order to try to get his point across. Meanwhile, yours truly was still struggling with pride issues and wasn't dealing too well with this kind of treatment as a new babe in Christ. God sometimes chooses to send someone in our lives to be like sandpaper. However, self-respect was something that had been drilled in my head since I was little and I was taught that you give respect in order to give it. It was a worldly instruction that seemed alright, but when put to the test in everyday circumstances – it failed miserably. Unfortunately, I stated something to my new supervisor that he felt was unacceptable and he eventually fired me.

My whole world was falling apart. I was becoming a product of society's philosophy. Finishing up my work and responsibilities, I drove my truck eastward on the St. George bridge. Suicide was racing through my mind big time as I thought my life was about to end. What hope did I have without my wife? After all, she was the only thing I ever really loved despite knowing little about what love was. These thoughts became intense and overwhelming. I realized that I needed some answers. Crying out in desperation; I told the Lord that I was either going to take my life or commit it to Him. I knew He had heard my cry when I felt everything negative that was built up in me being released. Later that day, I began reading a passage in psalms that states, "Commit yourselves unto the Lord; trust in Him also." This had to have been God's spirit ministering to me. He was putting a new song in my heart just like Psalm 40 says. This was nothing but a God-Incidence – not a mere coincidence. At that very moment, I knew my second mother Pat had been praying for me. What happened became so real and I'm reminded of that moment every time I sing "Amazing Grace." This was God's conversion power in that hour!

I remember one of my old co-workers Charlie, who worked side by side with me, daily shoving the gospel down my throat. Charlie was a thin, country man about my age at the time with a wife and two small children. After my experience, my first thought was go and tell him what had happened to me. I then heard a voice I had never heard in my life before. I knew it wasn't God because the voice was trying to dissuade me from telling Charlie, so I knew it had to be the Devil. I told this voice, "I listened to you for 29 years and I'm not listening to you anymore!" God must have really had something in store for my life for the Devil to come at me in the beginning in such a manner. Before this, I made a god out of Rock n' Roll music and many musicians! Isn't it amazing that we can be listening to the Devil's messages all of our lives and not even know it's him!

The Bible says 2 Corinthians 4:4 : He is the God of this world and has blinded the minds of them which believe not from seeing the Glorious Gospel of Jesus Christ! I was so blind that I couldn't see that the devil had me! When we have been set free out of the territory of the enemy, why would we ever want to go back? I've seen this happen to so many, but God changed my life miraculously. For me, there was nothing to go back to. The Scripture says that it is better if we were never even born than for us to betray Him and turn away from the Truth. When we read God's Word – especially in the beginning, we must allow Him to grasp us by His Holy Spirit. We must be willing to change whatever God is asking us to change. I was set free that day and ever since then, I've been free!

Now I had to grow, but who would know and show me the way better than Him? Sure, I sinned – but I always repented of it to stay on track! In every one of our lives as believers, it was the seed of the Word of God that brought us to this place of being born again of His Spirit! If God through His Word and by His Spirit puts us on the right path, can't we believe that it will keep us on that continued path that leads to life? Everyone that I have spoken to that fell into sin and backslid confirmed that it was because they departed from Word of God. What did the enemy come forth to steal? The Word of the Living God out of the hearts of men and women! Will we allow the enemy to steal the Abundant Life? No – because knowing our Creator is the Abundant Life.

Faith Adventures Episode 12
New Expectations With Little Faith

When I was working in Carrabelle, God had given me the ability to build a route as a bread vendor despite how small the town was. Little did I know that I would be faced with making a decision so soon regarding gambling. There were always two events that stuck in my mind about gambling. I remember my experience at a carnival earlier in my life at the age of twenty-two. I had a nickel or two and wanted to win my new girlfriend a bear. Much to my surprise, I pitched one right into the bowl and won the bear! I was so excited that I had won so quickly! There was a man there who was responsible for giving me my winnings. He was very gracious and also mentioned a bonus chance to win something even better. There was a barrel with numbered ping pong balls that I played, thinking I would win something better. I ended up losing twenty dollars! This was like playing the lottery, but I never had much luck winning. I had learned my lesson and told one of my co-workers about my experience the next day. I have never desired to play the lottery all the days of my life and even more so since Christ changed my life. I was reminded of the story about the Roman soldiers who gambled over the robe of Jesus and since then promised that I would have nothing more to do with that act.

At the age of twenty-seven, there was another event that I shall never forget. After a company meeting, I overheard the employees talking about playing poker. I only had a little bit of money, but not enough to go out to a nightclub and pick up women. I decided to play in hopes of winning the amount of money that I needed to go out and do what I wanted. After two hours of constant victory, I decided that

I had had enough and wanted to leave. The other players tried convincing me to stay, but I knew they just wanted a chance to win their money back; so I refused. After witnessing how upset they became, I never gambled much after that. I believe God used this to show me the reality of man's greed. As odd as it may sound, this is one of the very things my father warned me about even though he was practically an alcoholic his whole life.

One day, after working my Florida West Coast route for a little over a year; I received a letter from Flowers Baking Company commending me for winning the West Coast contest for increased sales volumes on a single route. In order to receive my prize, I was asked to come and pick it up at a resort on my day off. When I arrived along with the other winners, we were given a certain number of chips according to our accumulated sales. I remember receiving 84 chips. The head management team led us to the gambling tables where we could choose whatever game we wanted to play. Our goal was to win more chips so that we could use them to bid on prizes. Here I am a born-again Christian being faced with gambling once again! I didn't feel right in my spirit participating in this and even had one friend try to mislead me by saying that we were doing was not gambling. I told him that I didn't feel like this was what God wanted me to do. This may have brought conviction to my co-workers.

That night, I left that area and decided to just walk around the resort. I remember as I gazed up into the starry heavens, I could almost hear God say that He was well pleased in me taking a stand for Him. There were quite a few people there that asked me why I wasn't playing. I had a chance to tell them of how God had changed my life miraculously and bore witness of Jesus Christ to them. After speaking, one man who I believe may have been a professing Christian even took less than what he could have bid for with all the chips he accumulated. With my 84 chips – very little in comparison to most, I was able to get my wife a nice watch. I believed God blessed me in this way for taking a stand for Him.

Later on in my journey as a new believer in Messiah Jesus; I realized I was a chronic complainer. This was something I had developed into a habitual practice. One day, I was reading Philippians 2:4 that states: "Do all things without murmuring and disputing." (KJV). I knew that this was the same type of complaining that led many of the Hebrew children into destruction. I carefully reflected over these words and admitted to God in all honesty that I was struggling with that spirit. I took the time for a short, sincere prayer, asking the Lord to do whatever it took to change me. Even though, I later still found myself complaining regarding my responsibilities at work.

I had to meet a certain time schedule and was often requested to clean the shelves in my stores. I didn't like to be told something more than once – once was even often enough for me considering my attitude. One particular day however, a clerk at one of the stores received an alarming phone call. The clerk shouted, informing me of what was taking place at another store down the street that happened to be my next stop. She told me that there were gunmen there who had all of the people on the floor with guns to their heads! Had I complained about cleaning the shelves that day and left before completing them, who knows if that could have been me in the next store lying at gunpoint? I cried out to the Lord and thanked Him for showing me the importance of not murmuring. I immediately responded to the Lord and told Him that I would never complain again about my job.

God has a way of changing us if we are totally honest with Him. This truly was God's supernatural work that began in me. On another occasion, all the salesmen were asked to clean shelves. After our brief discussion, I eagerly asked where the cleaning liquids in order to get started. The vendors around me were amazed by my response and later asked, "What is it with you? Do you like to clean shelves?" This gave me the opportunity to share with them how God changed my attitude toward something I really didn't like to do in order to give glory to Him for what He had done.

God can change our negative attitude and replace it with a positive one through His process of deliverance. We just need to be willing to receive everything He says as a stepping stone to become the disciple He desires us to be. I've always believed that it has taken us all of our lives to become what we are, but to stay that way all of our lives speak volumes to the world and our Christian brothers and sisters regarding a sense of denial. We say things like, "God accepts me just the way I am; I don't need to change." We need to do everything wholeheartedly unto the Lord despite how we think or feel about things. We must come to the revelation that His change in us is for our welfare. It is not within our nature to change and sometimes there is pain involved in these changes. However, this is His process of yielding within us something to come out that will be fruitful and pleasing in His sight!

Faith Adventures Episode 13
God's Plan- Nothing Less Than Miraculous

March 1977 was the year I had lost my job in Carrabelle. There were only two types of employment opportunities that were available in the town. It was either the shrimping or the oyster industry. I never learned how to swim, so neither of these were options and wouldn't even pay enough to cover rent unless you had experience in those fields. I diligently sought God in prayer more than any time in my entire life. I was in a place of desperation and that's putting it lightly.

Shortly after losing my job, I decided to call Mr. Ellis, the supervisor that originally interviewed and hired me. He was a tall and well-built man, always ready for any problems that would arise either in the bakery or in the management of all the vendors down the whole West Coast of Florida. However, our conversation was very brief. With no promises and no job offers, I was left with no hope. He did permit me to come up to the company's headquarters in Thomasville, Georgia to speak to him during the time when the special meeting with all of the salesmen would take place. Thankfulness welled up in my heart regarding this opportunity, so much so that I invited Charlie to come with me on my journey. The trip took a couple of hours, so on the way, I sought Charlie's advice. Unfortunately, Charlie was of no help. Imagine that, my gospel shoving ex co-worker didn't have any answers for me. To my recollection, I don't even remember him suggesting that we pray. When I finally realized, I wouldn't get anything out of him, I began to seek the Lord on this matter. It was just Him and me now – something I wasn't accustomed to at this time in my life. My prayer was simply for God to work things out for me because of the dilemma I was now facing. I didn't know what would happen, but I was willing to put my trust in God.

As I approached the meeting with Mr. Ellis, I was quite nervous. A frightening thought crossed my mind as I sat in his office. Mr. Ellis recalled something that I already knew while sitting on the edge of my seat. I remembered his words so clearly: "It has been brought to my attention that you and Ray cannot get along." I had no defense so I just sat there listening. I was hoping some of the other negative things that I had done wouldn't get brought up in the conversation. Not knowing what was coming next; I embraced myself for the worse. Besides, there was already enough evidence gathered to find me guilty without even digging up other things.

To my amazement, Mr. Ellis told me about a route that was available in the Tallahassee Capital area. The route consisted of one, twenty-four-hour big chain store that was constantly busy to serve this fast, growing area. There were also about twenty other mom and pop stores added to this route. I had heard about these kinds of routes. Finally! A glimmer of hope emerged within me even though that wasn't the answer I anticipated. He told me all about this like it was my only other alternative. I don't know why, but naturally I should have jumped on the opportunity. Most people would have done the same, yet something inside was telling me that this was not the right choice. My wife was not around anymore to urge me into making a decision for our security. Therefore, I had no one to answer to but God. I know now that this was the Holy Spirit working on my behalf. I declined Mr. Ellis' offer and was not pressured on his part in any way to do otherwise. I thank the Lord that He knew it would have been too much for me in my early stages of walking with Christ.

According to 1 Corinthians 10:13, "For no temptation has overtaken and laid hold of you that is not common to man. But God is faithful and He can be trusted not to let you be tempted, tried and assayed beyond your ability and strength of resistance and power to endure, but with the temptation He will also provide the way out, that you may be capable and strong and powerful to bear up under it patiently." This basically means that God will not allow any more to come upon you that you can bear. I didn't know at that time this was a God-given revelation. He knows what we can bear even more than we do.

It wasn't long before Mr. Ellis mentioned one more possibility. They had just opened up a brand-new agency in the Tampa Bay area. Mr. Ellis explained to me that because the company was just breaking into this new frontier, there would be many challenges, but if I was willing to work hard and long hours – we would make a breakthrough in this new area of business. I've always welcomed these kinds of challenges because God had put this kind of spirit of perseverance in me. When I heard these words, it thrilled my heart beyond measure! I knew in my spirit this was what God wanted to happen. He also told me that the company would also be willing to cover all expenses in order to make this a reality. This was absolutely amazing considering that my termination from my job was now on my record. My thoughts for some time were that Ray was very unreasonable in his decision. Ultimately, I knew God worked on my behalf – there is no other explanation. It was another God-Incidence.

There is something that I have learned and have observed in the lives of many believers. God imparts such bountiful mercy by demonstrating His love towards us in the beginning of our walk-in Christ. Let this story and many stories to come in the future Faith Adventures be an encouragement to you to continue your adventure that God has purposed and planned for your lives. Enjoy your race in everything you go through and God will work for you.

Faith Adventures Episode 14
Have Faith – Despite Your Circumstances

My brother Kevin and I began packing up our belongings to head to Tampa for this new venture that God had opened up. I decided to inform Darlene that we were leaving Carrabelle. I shared my whole story with her of how God had worked everything out. She pleaded for me to bring her along, and as the forgiving person that I had become; I gladly took her. When God had gotten a hold of me, it appeared as if all of the sudden things were beginning to work out for my good – just like the Scripture says in Romans 8:28.

When we first arrived in Tampa, we beheld the sights. God had brought me to the ocean, a new town and a new job! I remember the first day I went to this new bread agency and to say the least, I was excited. One rather huge man by the name of Ron came up behind me placing some kind of rope around my neck and said, "We are going to straighten you out!"

I turned around to this man and replied, "God has already done that!" So, startled by my response, he backed away. This place was quite the challenge – it was full of heathens who all knew where I stood from the beginning. I was telling this agency from the start about Jesus Christ and how He had changed my life around.

Much to my amazement, Ray – my old supervisor walked in one day to the Tampa agency to visit from another nearby one. Ray was the supervisor that had terminated me shortly after I first came to believe in Christ. I believe he realized like many, my God was bigger than all of Flowers Baking Company put together. The company had given us a motel and all other expenses paid for about two weeks. The challenge now was to find a decent place to rent. Not only were we having trouble finding anything decent, but we couldn't find anything at all. This is when we decided to endeavor buying a brand new mobile home. The salesman we spoke with was very kind – at least up until he began talking to us regarding our financial state. When we left Carrabelle, there were still some payment obligations that we left outstanding.

When the salesman heard this, he literally laughed in our faces and said to us, "Do you really believe you are going to buy this trailer with all of the debt you are still facing?" We needed a loan at this time. Although he made a fool out of us, we trusted God and asked for him to submit the request anyway. Sadly, it had already gone through six different loan agencies and we were turned down, one by one. Meanwhile, I remember working very long, strenuous hours on a daily basis during the process and having to tell my family back at the motel every night that we weren't approved for the home. We were facing a crisis as new believers, so I did something that I had remembered my wife had done on several occasions. She would just pray and open up the Bible to wherever passage God led her.

I was ready to try anything out of desperation. I did this very thing for the first time in my Christian walk. I opened up to the story about Peter as he was attempting to walk across the water and lost faith! I believe God was speaking to me to let my wife know that God wanted us to not lose faith, but believe that He would see us through. The very next morning, I called my seventh loan agency. While dialing, I was already having doubts arise in my mind. After questioning whether or not we were approved for the loan, the woman on the phone replied, "Yes sir! You most certainly did!" She immediately began explaining how unbelievable our situation was and how everyone in the agency was talking about this miraculous loan all morning long! "Sir, this has never been done before throughout this agency's existence. We have to know how you did this because it's remarkable," she said. I simply told her that the Lord has done it for us. She responded, "It must be because it's never been done before to our knowledge!"

When we have experienced adventures like this in our lives, we never forget what God has done because He continues to amaze us. The Bible tells of how David was able to defeat the giant Goliath. When King Saul asked him, "How would he defeat the one who has defiled all the armies of Israel?" David's response should speak volume to us today! He told the King that God gave him the lion and God gave him the bear while attending and protecting his sheep. David defeated Goliath because he remembered his victories! Many of us have had victories, but so many of us have forgotten what God once did.

Faith Adventures Episode 15
Roots, Not Necessarily the Fruits

Back when I was still living in Carrabelle; I was attending this church under the Assemblies of God. Unfortunately, no one ever offered their friendship toward me nor was I trained up to teach and practice the biblical principles of discipleship. This was a task that I felt the denomination failed at miserably. Jesus taught that we are to make disciples, yet that seemed to be least in the church. A good friend of mine who was part of the pastoral leadership was even voted out of office because he was preaching the importance of our involvement in Kingdom work. This was not a surprise to me and I began discovering very quickly that some Christians were not who they professed to be.

This pastor eventually moved across the state to another location and my family actually helped him, his wife and his two sons in that process. We received his new address and paid visits to him, supporting the new ministry that God had given him. We spoke quite often together about the things of God because the Lord had put a hunger within me that couldn't be quenched. We became friends many years ago and still remain friends to this day. You will hear about his family in the future Faith Adventures. Shortly thereafter, I became a follower of the Old- Time Gospel ministry and received many good Biblical teachings while also receiving discipleship training through Jerry Falwell's ministry over the televised program.

Not too long after transitioning to Tampa, while attending a friendly fellowship called Hillsdale Baptist church – we were in search of a Pentecostal ministry in the area. I was still pondering on whether or not God was leading us in that direction. My younger brother Kevin had responded to a Sunday morning altar call to accept Jesus, but was never followed up with. Although I resorted to help him in his spiritual walk, the last one he wanted to hear it from was the one closest to him. We ended up leaving the church only to receive a follow-up call literally a month after we left. Within that same month, I was bowling one night and began witnessing to a man, unaware that he was a preacher. His name was Leonard; he liked the fact that I was witnessing to him in that type of atmosphere and stated that it should have been him witnessing to me.

I met his son Mike, who was a bit younger than me and we seemed to hit it off very well from the start. Pastor Leonard asked if my wife and I would like to come and visit the church. We did the following Sunday and could immediately sense a difference in this house of worship. It was not just a small congregation, but a family. The people seemed very genuine and I liked the preaching because it was more in depth regarding living a holy and righteous life. The Pastor from Hillsdale was very gracious when I explained to him that we were going elsewhere, but where was he or anyone else when it came to following up on the people? Some churches do not want to take responsibility for the people that the Lord brings their way. It's almost like giving a man a job without telling him what to do day after day. I believe that today there are many churches and ministries that do not teach the message of the Kingdom of God. While that message should teach us to obey His commandments, most of the messages today are only preaching grace. We must remember what God requires of us and as a church, we must be responsible with the Gospel and be careful with whom the Lord has entrusted to us to build up for His Kingdom.

Faith Adventures Episode 16
True Conversion-Looks on No Man

Shortly after my conversion we began to attend the Assembly of God church back in Carrabelle, Florida. Pastor Cameron Smith was my first pastor and partly a mentor. He was a very good biblical pastor and a man of integrity. He spoke many times on how we needed as believers to take the gospel out and do works of righteousness! This was probably why many people in his church were complaining about his preaching. They were not coming to terms with what God was saying through him. My wife and I heard what God was saying through him and we put into action God's Word spoken to us. I began to overcome my timidity and to become very friendly to just about anyone. I was told by many that people didn't like this, so I tried to listen to the Holy Spirit for direction in who to speak to. I had only one thing to say, and that was how God took me out of a great darkness and brought me into His Marvelous Light. This was my testimony that God had me tell for the longest time. I never shall forget how His Mercy poured down on me mightily!

At this time, we began to visit nursing homes, young people and people with mental and physical disabilities; the less fortunate that our Messiah Jesus spoke of. We knew they couldn't give back, so we went to see them with only a pure motive of love. They loved to see and hear Christ ministering to them through us every time we would visit them. I shall never forget the time, when we had not been there for some time that when we entered the door they all cheered upon our entrance!

One other home we were visiting while ministering, we heard quite a bit of screaming and commotion. The man in charge told us there was a lady in the next room that was crazy, and for us not to go near her. I stepped in her room alone and I could see they had her restrained in a high crib, but the top was open. At this early stage in my life in Christ I knew nothing of the demonic realm. One thing I knew for sure is that Satan had me no more, and there was no place I gave to him. I decided God's Spirit was leading me to bend over the top of her, to simply tell her that Jesus loves her. She began to raise her hand and I lowered my face into her crib; she raised her hand to hit me, but something stopped her from harming me. That was the love of Christ pouring His love into her through me. She knew I loved her and proved it to her with no fear in me showing her that love.

According to the pastor's confirmation of these facts, I believe we were the only ones at his church that were doing these works of righteousness. This same congregation would always testify how they loved God, but only by their lips, not from their hearts.

I remember I needed quite a few men to help to move a very heavy portion of my trailer to get set up to live and the first time hardly anyone showed up. The job was put off to a week later. When the next time came, again, no one showed up to help. They had assured me both times at the church that they would gladly be there. I learned something important very early in my walk as I had learned earlier in life; you can't depend on what men say they will do. So, there were from the very start many reasons, that I could have left the church. His own congregation had never helped him move, except one new brother in Christ. We, as a family, helped them to fill their U Haul.

The board of his church actually voted him out for reasons of convicting them, because they didn't want to be servants. The reality is that they probably trumped up other reasons for his departure. That sounds like what they did to Christ during his trial before He went to the Cross for all mankind.

Faith Adventures Episode 17
Prayer of Faith in The Right Place

We had just begun attending Malone Chapel in Tampa, Florida at this time. Pastor Leonard (remember, I met him in bowling alley, past Faith Adventures Episode 15) was a rather large man, but carried himself well. He was clean shaven and had that look of the preacher in a pinstripe suit. When he preached, he came right to the point of bringing people to the bull's-eye. This was a term preachers used to get right to the heart of the matter to target the man's heart. One of the first messages I received from Pastor Leonard was the story of Thomas. Many refer to Thomas as doubting Thomas, but if we look at this story in a different perspective it can speak volumes to us, spiritually speaking. When Messiah Jesus was speaking to Thomas, he was telling him that he was blessed by seeing, but how much more can we be blessed without seeing. This came about because he had missed the first visitation of the Messiah to the Disciples. In the account of John 20:19-29 NASB:

Verse 19: "When therefore it was evening, on that day, the first day of the week, and when the doors were shut where the disciples were, for fear of the Jews, Jesus came and stood in the midst, and saithe unto them, 'Peace be unto you.' V20: And when he had said this, he showed unto them his hands and his side. The disciples therefore were glad, when they saw the Lord. V21: Jesus therefore said to them again, 'Peace be unto you: as the Father hath sent me, even so send I you.' V22: And when he had saithe this, he breathed on them, and saithe unto them, 'Receive ye the Holy Spirit.'"

As I later studied this portion of Scripture in the original Greek, I discovered that this meant in the same sense of the Hebrew, that God breathed into Adam and he became a living soul. He promised on His return that they would receive the impartation of the Holy Spirit to live and abide in them forever. They had received and had become born from above (Born Again). The truth of the matter according to the Scriptures, was that no one could become born again until after Christ our Messiah had risen from the dead receiving his new resurrected immortal body by God the Father. John 7:39 NKJV states, "But this He spoke concerning the Spirit, whom those believing in Him would receive; for the Holy Spirit was not yet given, because Jesus was not yet glorified." Apostle John frequently speaks of Jesus being glorified, and it is nearly always in conjunction with his death, resurrection and return thereby to the Father (7:39; 12:16, 23, 28; 13:31, 32; 17:1, 5). Book of John

He also told something to His disciples that was very significant. He told them before He departed that it would be an advantage to them that another Comforter would come and live and abide within them forever. They could not understand what Messiah was saying until they received the Holy Spirit. None of us, not one can understand, not Thomas or anyone else until this work of God's Spirit was wrought within. If we say we have received the Holy Spirit but yet choose not to listen to that which God has supernaturally imparted into us; we have missed it. The Lord told us also that He would do even greater works than Him. It is the Christ working through us by the power of the Holy Spirit to bring forth impartation of His spirit to bring hope to others with the measure of faith that God has placed within us.

Verse 23: "Whose so ever sins ye forgive, they are forgiven unto them; whose so ever sins ye retain, they are retained. V24: But Thomas, one of the twelve, called Didymus, was not with them when Jesus came. V25: The other disciples therefore said unto him, 'We have seen the Lord.' But he said unto them, 'Except I shall see in his hands the print of the nails, and put my finger into the print of the nails, and put my hand into his side, I will not believe.' V26: And after eight days again his disciples were within, and Thomas with them. Jesus cometh, the doors being shut, and stood in the midst, and said, 'Peace be unto you.' V27: Then saith he to Thomas, 'Reach hither thy finger, and see my hands; and reach hither thy hand, and put it into my side: and be not faithless, but believing.' V28: Thomas answered and said unto him, 'My Lord and my God.'"

Now let's talk about Thomas, who wasn't there for this great event when Jesus made it plain to the disciples through the women to be there in Matthew 28:10. Just like Thomas, many of us are not in the place God wants us to be. When we, like Thomas, look upon what we need to see to believe, we are surely in the wrong place! Many that will be reading this are out in the wrong place. Are we out of God's Sanctuary missing the greatest event: Have we allowed man by his lifestyle and practices keep us out of the arena of worship? Are we persuaded by too many comments from others that have never really experienced a time of worship like the psalmist describes? Psalm 16:11 NKJV; "You will show me the path of life; In Your presence is fullness of joy; At Your right hand are pleasures forevermore."

Are we like a sheep gone astray and strayed away from good biblical teachings? Could it be we are no longer teachable and in many cases because of pride can't be reached? Do we think we have already arrived? Soon it will be forty years I've been in service to the Lord, and by His grace and strength through His Word I have missed very little. I have not arrived, but I'm sure enjoying the trip! God says He desires us to be in His dwelling place, the sanctuary. (Our local church).

We can miss His true impartation in the form of many baptisms and deliverance through His Body by being in some other place. Sure, we can experience a measure of His presence and workings outside the sanctuary. It is not near to what we can experience through the fullness of a formed body with Messiah formed within us; how God biblically has designed this to be. According to Paul's writings to the Colossians in Chapter 1:25, he was to make the Word of God fully known [among you]— In the following verses 26-27, he stresses verse 26; "The mystery of which was hidden for ages and generations [from angels and men], but is now revealed to His holy people (the saints)." Verse 27, "To whom God was pleased to make known how great for the Gentiles are the riches of the glory of this mystery, which is Christ within and among you, the Hope of [realizing the] glory. (AMP) The enemy will endeavor to keep you out of this place; the place God has placed believers in place for His will and Divine purposes.

When I first heard this story of Thomas, I was so moved by what Messiah Jesus said, Verse 29: "Because thou hast seen me, thou hast believed: blessed are they that have not seen, and yet have believed." Like Thomas, I haven't seen Jesus in His physical body. I believe He was speaking to me to not have to see anything to believe in Him in accordance to the Scriptures: "For we walk by faith, not by sight." 2Corinthians 5:7 God, by His Spirit, had me respond with a simple prayer. I prayed that I would not have to see anything to continue to believe on the One that had changed my life for all eternity. I believe God put me on that very path for close to forty years! This truly has been a humbling experience walking in His Light. He made this possible and with so much more to come. I'm always amazed day after day what He has to say to me and through me that He alone may be glorified in it all.

Faith Adventures Episode 18
God Places His Burden in me for Souls

We are still attending Malone Chapel and during this time I met Paul, an older preacher that I have come to know and respect. Anyone could see he desired to live a life of integrity and raised his two sons, Wally and Jonathon, to live in the same manner. Paul began an intense weekly bible study of the Book of Revelation. I was excited to begin this study to learn, what I thought, would be the deeper things of God. While reading, and discussing the churches that Messiah Jesus addressed, I underlined in my Bible that this particular church, Ephesus, had lost its first love. I knew at this same time what God had placed in me was more of a hunger for His Word, and learning to be the disciple He desired me to be.

I didn't know much then, but I knew in my heart I wanted others to see Jesus for themselves. I had received this first love of my Messiah in the beginning and it has remained fresh within me all the days of my life in Christ. Something happened to me as we were in the Book of Revelation studies. This was beyond my comprehension, what God was doing in me. God was having me reflect not so much on the symbols and things in our natural mind's you couldn't comprehend anyway, but on the affects these things were having on the earth and mankind. How many books have been written with incorrect interpretations on Revelation? This seems to take you down an endless path! Many today are reflecting on anti-Christ and not reflecting on Christ to be everything He has designed us to be. The will of the Lord is to be His disciple and in times (usually years) grow and mature to be everything He desires us to be. This is when we have begun to understand this scripture passage. He that does the will of our Father will enter up into the Kingdom of God, work here and now and the Kingdom according to God's Redemption plan later.

There was one thing that was taught according to The Book of Daniel that strengthened my belief more in the living Word of God. This was the dream of the King Nebuchadnezzar. This was an historical and biblically true account with a vision of a statue beginning with Babylon down to other kingdoms to the ultimate Kingdom of God. This was probably the first time I really enjoyed history and could see that all these kingdoms historically lined up with God's Word. If something had happened thousands of years ago and throughout the Scriptures the fulfillment of these has happened, how could we not be moved? The real excitement is in reading and seeing what God has already done. If our excitement is only in looking for the things to come, our excitement is not gleaned from hungering and thirsting for His Righteousness now.

When we eat a good regular nutritious meal, we are filled and satisfied; it is something our body is accustomed to, and this is how our body speaks to us. If we go out eating something foreign we are not accustomed to, sometimes we don't know what the effects will be! Then our body speaks to us that this was not good for us. The daily Word of God, discovering the truth is like that daily meal that is fulfilling and very satisfying. The other things that are foreign to our body are like seeking the mysteries of God, outside of what God has been saying and what He is truly saying in accordance to His infallible Word. This kind of hunger and satisfaction prepares us for what is yet to come in our lives! Romans 8:35 KJV states that there is nothing that can separate us from His love. We can choose to separate ourselves in our own rebellion towards God. The verses to follow verse 38-39, "For I am persuaded that neither death nor life, nor angels nor principalities nor powers, nor things present nor things to come."

One day, I pondered on the things to come. We don't know what tomorrow holds, but we know Who holds tomorrow. The Lord also told us not to worry about tomorrow because today has enough trouble of its own. When I was beginning to see what mankind would have to endure and go through, God put a burden in my heart in a greater manner for souls for His Kingdom's sake! If God puts a burden on us in this manner, He will give us that hunger and thirst along with this. This is so we can share the love of God that He has shed abroad in our hearts. 2Corinthians 2:15-16 NKJ; "For we are to God the fragrance of Christ among those who are being saved and among those who are perishing. Verse16 To the one we are the aroma of death leading to death, and to the other the aroma of life leading to life."

Faith Adventures Episode 19
My First Message Preached

I'm still at Malone Chapel and I was asked to preach my first message. This message had to do with the Importance of the Word of God daily in the believer's life. Every time I have the opportunity to preach, throughout all the years God has always given me, the inspiration of the Holy Spirit told me the message He would have me to preach. This first time was no different, bringing forth this message with a continual burning in my bones; God did something profound in me that I continually proclaim to this day.

God gave me the illustration of a carpenter going to work without his proper tools, causing him not to do his job effectively. He forgets one of the most important tools a man of his trade uses. You guessed it: he forgot his hammer! He has traveled hundreds of miles, not even a thought that he had forgotten the most important tool to get started with. He has put himself in a dilemma, leaving without the most important tool to complete the task. He attempts to use his shoe or other tools as a hammer and frustrates himself throughout the whole day with the same success.

When man first invented the tools for the best completion he knew by experimentation in time what would be the outcome. Do we know what the outcome will be for our lives? Are we content in who we are? Better yet, are we content in what God has done in creating us? If we don't like what God has done how can we expect others to like us? We can be well satisfied in the Godly design He has made us in and actually like ourselves. This is not because we have done anything special in bringing this about. This is because the Father has bestowed His love upon us in abundance. God says that we are fearfully and wonderfully made. When we are content in what God has already done and is presently doing we are well on our way to a life full of Godly contentment. Our Creator knows better than we will ever know what we need and desires the very best for us.

The inventor (creator) of the automobile knew in the process of his invention, what it would take to operate the vehicle and has provided us with instructions. The plan was designed for many diversities of vehicles. This is why it is so important to learn the basic instructions. Most of us treat God no differently than an automobile manual. Again, most of us, when we purchase a new vehicle we will look throughout the whole manual. Some of us, when we receive our first Bible we will possibly read the whole thing in a year's time. We are so captured by all this new knowledge like all the new accessories in our automobile. Like the vehicle manual, we put our Bible away unless we need it in an emergency. Some of us may say that we have read the Bible. Like the manual, we think we know everything that it says and our pride springs up thinking we no longer need it, like we no longer need the Word of the Living God, to operate. The only time most of us look to the manual is when we are in trouble. Because we have not looked to Him all along, pride will keep us away even in times of our greatest troubles. Psalm 119.28 KJV, "My soul melteth for heaviness: strengthen thou me according unto thy word." D.L. Moody said, and I quote "Either sin will keep you from this Book or this Book will keep you from sin."

The same way we need oil for the engine to run properly, we need the oil of the Holy Spirit operating each and every day of our lives. We never know when or how often we will face frustrations in everyday living. I would like to share several experiences to enlighten what I am trying to say. I was working for a taxi-cab company and I got a flat tire. I only knew to do what I had experienced at other times with a flat tire. However, I could not loosen the lug nuts. I thought I was too weak to do it. A policeman stopped to assist me and he was very strong and husky, but he could not loosen the lug nuts either. I called the owner of the vehicle. He said that if I would turn the lug nuts the other way that would do it. It baffled me and I argued with him, like he didn't know what he was talking about. To my surprise they came off very easily when I tried his suggestion in frustration.

Too many times we argue with our Creator and this is what makes life hard on us. The flat tire is a good example of what we usually do. I wanted to do it my way. Instead, like many of us, I failed to go first to the owner, the Creator. Jesus said in Matthew 11:28-30 NASB, "Come to Me, all who are weary and heavy-laden and I will give you rest. Take My yoke upon you, and learn from Me, for I am gentle and humble in heart; and You Shall Find Rest For Your Souls. For My yoke is easy and My load is light." This means that when we submit to the Creator and His authority, life will come easier. It will be much easier than we think. When we truly have seen this we are well on our way to this journey to Godly contentment.

God has given His Word to all mankind and especially the sons and daughters of His Kingdom. We must be found faithful in doing all we know to do in accordance with His Word and He Alone knows the outcome. Messiah Jesus told His disciples that it was not for them to know the outcome when they asked about the things of the coming Kingdom.

Joshua 1:8 MSG states, "And don't for a minute let this Book of the revelation be out of mind. Ponder and meditate on it day and night, making sure you practice everything written in it. Then you'll get where you're going; then you'll succeed. Haven't I commanded you? Strength! Courage! Don't be timid; don't get discouraged. God, your God, is with you every step you take."

Too many of us believers have despised His Word and His teachings. As believers, we would never think of despising His Word by displacing it, putting it aside or disregarding it. Hebrews 10:28 states that they despised Moses law which was then and still today remains to be The Word of the living God! According to Matthew 5:14, Jesus said He didn't come to destroy it but to fulfill the law!

We have been given the right tools, but it's our responsibility to use them, not to displace or replace them with something else like Christian music and Christian preaching and teachings. There are many that Jesus spoke of that would speak things that would be on their lips, but their heart was far from them. They fall short of this, when their life and preaching is measured by the whole counsel of God. We have disregarded His Word when we take the word of a mere man, instead of God's All Inspiring Word. According to the Word of God we have made either man or woman our idols.

I always try to write as the Holy Spirit leads and directs me, so all of this message may have not been imparted in my first sermon. This is all the truth and we all must come to terms with the truth that can set us free. I'm only the newspaper boy, but you need to read the most important news God has brought down to man since He created the whole Universe. I heard one evangelist say, "Our eyes are made for the Word of God" and I never forgot that.

One day a little girl saw a book on a high shelf and couldn't get to it. She asked, "What book is this mommy?" Mommy said this, honey, is God's Holy Word that He brought down to all mankind. The little girl responded "Mommy, we need to give this book back to God because we have never used it!"

Faith Adventures Episode 20
God Given Vision for the Lost At All Cost

God was bringing me to more of an understanding that Tampa was the place He sent me to be a witness for Him. God had put such urgency in my spirit to reach the lost at any cost. In the beginning when I was given a route as a vender, I sought the Lord in prayer on how I could be a more effective witness on behalf of my Lord and Savior, Jesus Christ. God was calling me to this new task. This was one of the first visions I had received from the Lord. God showed me actors in a play and this represented us as believers in Jesus Christ. Then, He showed me the audience watching the play. He told me that the audience represented the world of unbelievers. God was saying that unbelievers and in some cases believers are watching us. God was speaking into my spirit to simply give out a greeting to let them know like the audience that we are followers of Jesus Christ. The type of greeting a person received during the Bible era demonstrated their status in society, so the scribes and other elite loved effusive greetings (Matt 23:7). Jesus' point was that such greetings should be given to strangers and even enemies, not just their fellow disciples.

Just like the actors revealing their identities, we need to in some way to let the world know we are Christians not only in word, but in deed. The Bible says we are to tell about the things of God with our lips as well as to tell the wonderful works of God, according to the Psalms. In the New Testament, we are to be living epistles and to breathe out life to those on a death road. This truly was me before I knew Christ, a man without hope. It is recorded in many of the letters of the Epistles that greetings were given to many of the brethren.

As I continued to meditate on what I believe God was revealing to me to say, "Have a nice day." Anyone, I thought could say this. God put it on my heart to say: "Have a nice day and may God be with you or God Bless you!" This became a habitual greeting to practically everyone Christ through me came in contact with. The Word says that our every conversation should become of Christ Jesus. This word, conversation, means in the original language talking, but also conducting our lives in such a manner that all things are pleasing to our Heavenly Father.

The Bible says we are to live up to our Master's commandments when we are with Him as well as not being in His company. This word was given to the masters on a job that were given authority over their servants. I went away for the weekend to Daytona to see my friend Pastor Smith and I had a free afternoon and for the first time since I was saved, decided to go to a movie theatre. God was doing something in my very beginning walk with Christ. Before I knew Christ, I loved to go to the theatre to see the newest movies and even some adulterous type movies. In our day, pornography was getting the monthly Playboy edition and attending these pornography type movies. Incidentally the Playboy calendars were soon trashed as God's conviction soon worked on me.

The very first movie I went to see was Smoky and the Bandit. As I was listening, practically every other word was a word cursing our Father in Heaven and His Son. I immediately left that theatre and never walked back in another one until there were actual Christian films. It was a long time waiting for such films. In the Christian film, "Time Changer" a preacher is brought into the year 2000 and from the 1890's. He was not only faced with the time change but witnessed the spiraling down of morality. When we are truly born again and God's Holy Spirit is active in our lives, we will no longer desire the things of this world. My testimony and I believe this should be all of our testimonies, is that we have come out of this great darkness into His marvelous light. There has been a transformation so radical in a sense that we never lived that life before.

I had many other conversations and God by His Spirit had me speak these things into unbelievers' lives. God had begun to give me the ability through His wisdom to turn any conversation into the gospel. I knew it was Him, not me because they would say to me from time to time that they would never talk to anyone before about religion. They knew it was God speaking through me and I was always amazed about the things that God would say. God knew what they needed to hear so He used me as His vessel to speak into their lives. Every time this would happen I would be humbled that God would use a nobody like me. I learned later what God by His Spirit had me doing was in accordance to the Scriptures. 1 Peter 4:11 says, "If any man would speak, if any man would minister, let Him minister and speak the oracles of God that Christ alone would be Glorified." When we trust God to give us the Words to say, the Father said over 2,000 years ago that He would give us the Holy Spirit and would give us the remembrance of whatever He said (John 14:26). We just need to be the participators of meditating on His Word and asking Him by His strength to do all things He has asked of us. When I first saw this, I got excited realizing it wasn't all up to me, but I could believe that He had promised this and the Word says all of His promises are true. Even the Old Testament says that not one Word of His has failed.

We are the ones that have failed God to believe that He could not do everything He has promised. God was beginning to impart to me biblical revelation. Messiah Jesus also said, "I Am the Bread of Life and He who partakes of Me will live." In several accounts, He also said; "Man shall not live on bread alone but by every Word that comes from His mouth." (Matthew 4:4) In Exodus 16:4, God said that He would rain bread from Heaven for them and He did, day after day. He also said that they should gather a day's portion every day that they may walk in His instruction. Does not God's Word teach us to walk in His instruction day by day? The KJV Bible says to gather at a certain rate which actually means in Hebrew to receive revelation as they were gathering. The reason that the majority were not receiving revelation is because they were trying to understand with their own understanding. This reflected back to what they had already experienced, bringing them to complain and not be thankful for God's daily provision.

One time when I went on vacation for a week, I heard that my supervisor was going to question everyone, believers as well as unbelievers, that I served on my route whether they would rather I preach to them, or not. All he heard from them was that "he doesn't preach to us." My customers were asking me when I returned why would this supervisor would do such a thing? We know why; Satan was using him to try to destroy God's witness in my life and rid me of my job, no doubt. I remember one time our supervisor was chastising my new brother in Christ about witnessing; the same thing that God had me doing. I stepped in and told my supervisor: If you come speaking to me in this manner, I'll tell you that this job means nothing to me in comparison to what I'm going through. At one point, they were saying to me; our company is a Christian company and you need to conduct yourself like us. I went into the supervisor's office and boldly said to him; "I'm going to tell you what Jesus told Pilate: 'Unless God gives you the Authority you can't get rid of me!'"

I did this in boldness in the fact that God sent me there and I would be there until it was God's timing for me to leave. I can say this because I knew God put me there and I was going to stay. I would like to say that if God has put you on your job; He will keep you there until He says it's time to go. I had a miraculous intervention in a later faith adventure to come.

I want to say again, I was a very hard and conscientious worker and I was hardly ever on the clock, and the management said that I had more potential in my little finger than all the men they have seen doing the same job. This is a vital part of our testimony that we work for the Glory of God with all our hearts! When we do our work, whatever it may be, if we truly love Him and He has made a change in us, we will do all things heartily unto our Lord. In future Faith Adventures there will be testimonies of these very things.

Faith Adventures Episode 21
Received Baptism-Speaking the Word of God with Boldness

For some time now and until this very day, God baptized me in accordance with Acts 4:31 KJV, "And when they had prayed the place was shaken where they were assembled together and they were all filled with the Holy Ghost and they spoke the Word of God with boldness." This baptism made quite a change in their lives because soon after they demonstrated that their life was not their own or anything they possessed.

This is also where the room was shaken, but they received the Baptism of the Holy Spirit of speaking the Word of God with boldness. I had received this baptism of fire at Malone Chapel at an altar of prayer by faith prior to this time period. 1 Kings Chapter 19, there is no doubt Elijah had received something similar when he thought he was alone. God spoke to him that there were seven thousand more liken unto him. He could not see any evidence of this other than Elisha his predecessor, but because God said there was; we can be assured of this Truth. There probably could have been multitudes of books written of these men. God said there were seven thousand then so how much more should we believe there are even more today. In my whole lifetime, I have barely met seven. Sometimes we think that we are the only ones like this because of our own experiences, but we are only limiting God of what He is doing today because His ways and thoughts are so much higher than ours.

Some years ago, I went to a different Assembly of God church with a friend of mine. They gave an invitation and it was to receive the Baptism of the Holy Spirit in the form of speaking in tongues. This was all new to me with the exception of hearing individuals speaking in some unknown language. I went forward and I was praying that if it was God's will for me to have it at this time; He would give it to me. One of the leaders heard me praying and was trying to coax me into this experience. When I said that I'm praying about this matter, he continued to try to push me into this experience. The pastor saw what was going on and gave me a dirty look, not a Christ-like behavior. I came to realize that you can't be part of them unless you play by their rules, so to speak.

Some years later I was going through such a hard time of my wife's departure, all I wanted to do was be in His presence because I loved being in His presence. I heard about a tent camp meeting going on in my area, which was Pentecostal. I wasn't too familiar with these kinds of meetings; however, I went frequently because I believed my antidote was being in His presence and worshipping Him. I'm not a lot into "feelings" so it was not something that made an impact on my life. God said to me sometime later, "Feelings cannot bring forth real faith, but faith can bring forth real feelings." (God's Refreshings)

Soon after I left the meeting, God spoke to me as I was witnessing to someone. God said, "What you received tonight is not enough to withstand all the opposition that is yet to come." That which God had done before was more than enough, the baptism of fire of God through me speaking His Word in boldness. This is not to say that there is no such thing as the gift of tongues. In the upcoming Faith Adventures, God showed me by speaking to me that this impartation is real also.

Many years later, I married a Pentecostal lady that God brought us together in the coming faith adventures. The church I was part of at this time required their minister go before a church denominational board to renew your license for ministry. The very first question they asked me was concerning this gift of tongues. They said they knew I married a Pentecostal lady. They asked me if she spoke in tongues. I sought quickly from the Lord the answer to give them. I replied "How would I know? She speaks in Spanish." Everyone laughed. God sure has a sense of humor!

Faith Adventures Episode 22
God's Continued Call for the Lost at All Cost

I waited on the call designed for my life for seven years. God didn't speak to me like most of us would think, in speaking to us in accordance to some kind of call. Most of us with expectations would be looking for God to speak to us in accordance to one of the Offices. I was driving up north to Maryland and I was calling on God and waiting to hear from Him. God said to me something in accordance to His Word, "You are the seed planter and throughout your ministry, will come great men, in their eyes you will not be great, but in My eyes, you will be even greater!" Everyone knows the name of Billy Graham, with very few exceptions. Who knows the man that greatly influenced his life? No one, but maybe him and a few could name his name. This unknown will be known as great in God's Kingdom if he kept walking in the Lord's will all the days of his life.

As far as I can remember back since God first touched my life, I had a burden in my heart for the lost. I knew what God had done for me, and I wanted everyone to know. The problem was that I was shy. I was so shy all throughout high school; I hadn't ever spoken to a girl throughout my school days. I felt frozen for some reason when I would be around the opposite sex. I had my share of crushes, but no one ever knew but me and of course, God. One of my biggest nights approached me in my senior year of school, but I never uttered a word to a girl to ask them out to the senior prom.

When we first came to Tampa, we were going to several churches and one pastor of a fairly large Baptist church actually came to my home to visit me. During this same time period; I was bowling one night and I was speaking to another pastor, not knowing he was a pastor. In our conversation, he was telling me about his church and invited me. We decided to go because I wasn't sensing God in any way remaining in the large Baptist church. This was kind of out of the ordinary because I was listening to and being discipled by Jerry Falwell, who was as Baptist as they come.

You might say God was leading and directing me in another way. This church was of the holiness persuasion and talked about a powerful baptism, something that I wasn't hearing in other church circles. I do not remember the entire message, but it was about the Baptism of the Holy Spirit in speaking the Word of God with Boldness. Acts 4:31 says: "And when they had prayed, the place where they had gathered together was shaken, and they were filled with the Holy Spirit and began to Speak the Word of God with Boldness." In verse 29, "And now Lord take note of their threats, and grant that your bond-servants may speak your Word with all confidence."

When I was going through the most difficult times in my life, I decided to be around believers and attend camp meetings that I heard about. One night, the evangelist prayed over me to receive the gift of speaking in tongues. I welcomed and received the experience of this baptism. To this day, I know this is not the baptism I was to receive in its fullness. I remember after leaving this uplifting meeting. This is what tongues does; for the believer edifies himself. I have approached many men to tell my testimony of how God changed my life miraculously. I couldn't count the times God just had me give my testimony to many people. There are a lot of us that just don't know what to say, as I had experienced many times. I would continue telling my testimony and God used this tremendously. I encourage anyone that is reading this that if you don't know what to say, just simply tell your testimony and it will go a long way. God said to me this very night that which I received tonight is not enough to withstand all the opposition I was yet to receive in being His witness. The Baptism of Boldness is more than enough to withstand anything that comes your way.

I received this Baptism of Speaking the Word of God with Boldness that day. You do not hear this message preached in church circles today to my knowledge. Later, I received the biblical evangelism plan as a revelation to me by His Spirit imparted by God. This is in accordance to 1Peter 4:11, "Whoever speaks, [let him do it as one who utters] oracles of God; whoever renders service, [let him do it] as with the strength which God furnishes him abundantly, so that in all things God may be glorified through Jesus Christ (the Messiah). To Him be the glory and dominion forever and ever (through endless ages). Amen (so be it)." Now couple this verse with John 14:26, "But the Comforter (Counselor, Helper, Intercessor, Advocate, Strengthener, Standby), the Holy Spirit, Whom the Father will send in My name [in My place, to represent Me and act on My behalf], He will teach you all things. And He will cause you to recall (will remind you of, bring to your remembrance) everything I have told you."

What happens to many of us believers is that we get caught up in these man-devised evangelism plans. That's okay, but if we are not allowing the Spirit to speak through us, we are not much different than a worldly salesman. One time, a salesman came to my home and God had me speaking to him and God had him so captured he said he almost forgot what he came to sell me. Remember, the Bible says as you read these things to be done that God would be glorified through His son, Jesus Christ.

Faith Adventures Episode 23
Supernatural Boldness in Word and in Song

Shortly after, we decided to go on the honeymoon we never had. My wife and I purchased tickets to board a Bahamas Cruise. We stayed in a motel the night before and went out to enjoy a patio type breakfast. We met a younger couple who were also going on this same cruise. In our conversation, I brought up how Jesus Christ had recently changed my life, but they were not about to continue this conversation. From their reaction, you could see this was not what they expected to happen. When we saw them on the cruise they seemed to turn away several times to go in another direction. With the new baptism, I had received, God was prompting me to speak to practically everyone on the cruise. I knew I had received something supernaturally to cause me to talk to everyone in sight!

On these cruises, everyone usually participates in everything they offer. There was one thing every one of us was agreeable to; food was available all the time and I was always there to partake of all these delicacies. One night, they had a worldly comedian, but he had a filthy mouth. We chose not to participate in this experience, but we were the only ones to walk out. The rest of the audience just went along with everything that was happening. Reminded me of what many say; everyone is doing it. We were not, so everyone was not doing it. I told them I would never take a vacation from the Lord. I met believers from all over the world there, and it seemed that's like what all of them were saying.

I remember how professing Christians would tell me the reason they didn't share about Christ was because they were on vacation. This was their justification in acting just like the world. They were drinking and gambling, with no thought God was watching it all. I heard they were one night conducting a gong show. I asked if I could enter to play the song the Lord gave me. They said that wasn't a problem. Singing and playing the guitar is all I ever wanted to do, but God obviously had another plan. They all came to the show that night, drinkers and gamblers, not what you would call a church atmosphere. There were about six contestants and they were very good and they completely shut them down by gonging them. My first thoughts were that they were about to crucify me.

My song was, *I know I'm Bound for Heaven* which I had written. Now, I was as nervous as a jaybird because this was out of my league. I played the guitar and sang the song and to my amazement, I didn't get gonged. This was the first song I wrote by God's inspiration and had a sense that God was doing this through me with God's Spirit all over me. The Master of Ceremonies got up and said, "I hope we are all bound for Heaven." The most profound thing happened the next day. The same couple that we had met prior to the cruise and saw during the cruise approached us and told us "we heard your song last night and we want you to know that we feel the same way." This was the greatest thing God did for someone and used me, the one, who could hardly play a lick. This was God working through me and all I can do is give God Alone all the Glory. When we saw them on the remainder of the trip they just couldn't keep away from us.

We were cruising back on the last day, coming into the Miami port. All the people were singing, still enjoying the trip to the very end. As soon as we docked everyone sighed that the cruise was over. I spoke out boldly to the crowd. The trip is never over when your life has truly been changed by Jesus Christ.

Faith Adventures Episode 24
Back to My Old Grounds – With New Grounds

Just the thought of going back up north where I grew up was rather frightening. I had thoughts racing through my mind that all my friends would laugh at me. I had never been really serious about anything in life. I remember when I told the gang I was going to Florida they all laughed, thinking I was joking. Could I expect from any of them less, knowing I joked about everything and never took life seriously? You might say they began to believe I meant something I said for the first time in my life.

There were other times when we all would agree and make choices and in what I remember. This was the crowd following event in most cases. One night, I went astray to another club which was little farther away. I told them about the new chicks and the different music and they seem to like what I was saying. After I told them about this new place, they agreed with me they would go there if I went with them to our usual hangout. I agreed to go, thinking they would keep their word, but when that Saturday night arrived they decided not to meet with their agreement. I saw what was happening. You either went along with the crowd or be left out. I decided to go to this new scene I had experienced and told them I was going with them or without them alone. That's what happened and I have learned to go it alone a lot. This is a part of us becoming an individual.

I had a very close friend Tim that when he got a new pair of threads he was bragging about how cool were these. Then I would go out and buy an identical pair and would try to impress him, but with no success. Through these experiences, I was learning to be an individual the way God designed us to be. To follow the crowd is easy and can lead us on the broad road to destruction.

To my surprise, but not totally, they didn't laugh at me, but said it was well for me, but not for them, at least at this time of thrills in their lives. I went to every one of my old friends to tell them boldly how Jesus Christ had changed my whole outlook on life and told my testimony because at this time I wasn't very Scripturally versed. God had me tell them I was just making a fool out of myself in all our partying together in the past, but now I have chosen to be His fool.

There was one younger girl in the family of one in the gang named Terri, a sister by birth. I had the opportunity to share with her my testimony and whatever God had me say to her by His Spirit like I had with all my other friends. I was not leaving any stones unturned. A few years later, I was visiting her sister and her son's which were all little ones from one of my best friends Don broken marriage. She said that she had to tell me something very important about her sister Terri. It seemed very urgent for her to convey this message to be given to me about the past. She said that Terri said when you were speaking to her she really didn't want to hear it and was trying to get away from me within her own thinking. Terri said this is what she needed to hear, but she didn't know it at the time. She said you tell Norman to keep on doing what he is doing because my life is changed today because he was faithful.

I also visited another part of our gang, but a little younger. My friend Johnny had become a drunkard for many years because he lost his teenage sweetheart in a car accident. Though he was drunk, he was listening to me and was drawing the cross and the accident of his girlfriend which at that time and for some time never came to terms with this big blow in his life like so many. In Faith Adventures to come you will see a real turnaround of Johnny, but a sorrowful trail to arrive to this place.

Faith Adventures Episode 25
Washington for Jesus a Must – Faith of Michael Abraham

I had been working now for Flowers Baking Company for about three years at this time. I heard about an event in Washington called "Washington for Jesus" and I believe it was 1980. Right away, I notified my supervisor that I wanted to go to this event and gave him plenty of notice. This is the first event like this that was happening on a large scale that I knew of. There were about 3/4 of a million believers that were about to gather in Washington to come to pray and Worship the King of Kings and Lord of Lords. My wife and I were so excited about this trip to Washington.

The time was drawing near, just a week before we were to leave. Something happened at our agency that was a very unusual occurrence. One of my co-workers, I believe his name was Ken, was very disgruntled about something. As he was loading his truck, he got so upset that morning that he walked off the job. I had never seen him in this kind of mood, the whole time we worked together. The supervisor was upset and came to tell me some bad news that because of this man's actions, it doesn't look like you are going to be able to go on the vacation that you planned because we are short a man. I responded in faith and told him in the spirit of boldness, face to face that I was going!

He looked at me like I was crazy and continued telling me that there was no way with the current situation. I responded back to him and said in faith: "I don't know how I'm going to go but I'm going." He walked away, wagging his head, probably not expecting this response. I earnestly prayed about this, just knowing in my spirit that this is what God wanted me to do and although it seemed like an impossible situation; I put it in His Hands. I worked all day just believing God was going to do something, but I didn't know what.

I came in later than usual and as I was finishing up my paper work, which too many times would take a long time because of computer errors. (This is something that I quite frequently prayed daily would work out in an ethical manner.) I remember my friend Ron (remember the man I first met at the agency?) one other night was getting totally frustrated over his paper work not working out. I just said simply to him: "Have you prayed about this?" He lifted up his head and in unbelief said: "Pray about this?", in a skeptical manner, but he agreed to pray and it shocked him that it worked out. He said, "Wow, if I would have known it was this easy, I would have prayed all along." After that day he always took it to our Father and it always worked out.

Then all of a sudden Ken walked in, speaking with our supervisor. He was pleading to get his job back and the supervisor took him back on. I believe God orchestrated this whole matter, so we could go to Washington! To say the least, we were excited about what God did. Now we are on the road and we saw a hitchhiker named Michael Abraham, so we felt compelled to pick this stranger up. We picked him up in South Carolina, south of the border. He told us that he had been part of a mission for some time in Ft. Lauderdale. We began speaking to him about our Savior and he seemed very open. He told us he was going to Boston, Massachusetts. We told him that we were stopping over at Jerry Falwell's church in Lynchburg, Virginia to attend church. He said that he would like to join us. My wife tried to fix him up as good as possible as he was dressed in tattered clothes! So, as we entered this big church I didn't know what to expect.

Much to my surprise, they treated this man like he had a three-piece suit on and that really impressed me the first time visiting this big church. In our communication, we found out more about the college on the mountain and Michael Abraham had a desire the next day to visit this college. We asked if they possibly knew of any good churches in the area of town where he lived? They told him about one right in his area of town.

We were in route for Washington and he wanted to go with us to be a part of this also. The night before the big meeting at the mall in Washington there was a meeting in a nearby stadium, which I had remembered going to attending a rock concert in my past life. The artists were the Allman Brothers and the Grateful Dead. That night, I couldn't tell you who the preacher was, but he gave an altar call for many to come forward. Michael Abraham asked my wife to ask me if I would go with him. I said sure without any hesitation, but as I'm going forward I couldn't help thinking about how these people must have thought I was getting saved also. It didn't matter to me what anyone thought, if it meant for another soul to be in God's Kingdom.

A volunteer talked to Michael Abraham explaining to him what he had just done. I was jumping up and down in my spirit for what God just had done! My wife gave him her own personal Bible to help him in his journey. The next day we were all rejoicing and praying and celebrating Jesus because of what God had done in our brother's life. They asked us to become part of a march around Washington to be witnesses unto the Lord and gave us some tracks. Now Michael also wanted to take part in this, because of the excitement he now saw in his new life in Christ! His desire to witness for the Lord all over Washington was unusual for a new convert. It was a wonderful event, but to us Michael Abraham was the main attraction!

We told Michael we were only going as far as Maryland to visit my friends and relatives. So we began to pray about him getting a ride to Massachusetts. We knew that the event had split us separately into our own states so we went to the Massachusetts section. We only spoke to a few and then in speaking to this one man he responded, "If you found me within this great crowd, then that means I need to take him home which is only twenty miles from my destination." God was working out all things for his good and no doubt God's purpose for his life because we never saw him again. We prayed and believed that which God had begun in him, would be furthered until the time Christ was to come in accordance to Philippians 1:6.

Faith Adventures Episode 26
Glorying in My Flesh- God's Thorn

This is something that I would say is God's Kingdom work within in His delivering power!

Every morning, the first thing I do is to meditate on His Word and be in Prayer. Reading the Word of God is actually another form of prayer because we are allowing God to speak to us. The passage I was reading this particular morning was 2 Corinthians 12 verses1, 4-7 and 11. These are the verses that God ministered to me very powerfully. Now Paul had received an abundance of revelations from God and was concerned in glorying in his own flesh. He was concerned on how men would focus on him like a god and he had to humble himself from being exalted above measure. As I was meditating on this portion of Scripture, God began to speak to me. God told me that this was what I was doing, glorying in my own flesh. To my knowledge, I had not received any kind of revelation at all in this manner. As I continued to meditate on this very important matter that God was showing me; God by His Holy Spirit was reminding me of a particular brother.

This brother Frank was sharing with me many things that God had said and was doing and I would respond and say, "Oh yes, I was the one that told you these things." God was showing me something very powerful; I was taking credit for what God was doing and saying out of me. This was another way that God was saying I was glorying in my own flesh. This was God bringing deliverance to me, because I responded in godly repentance. I prayed that I would never again take credit in any way for what God speaks to me and through me.

I know today because of God's Spirit, conviction was upon me, it prepared me for the days to come. Anytime to this day, when my friends and others try to recognize me, I will always give the Glory to God for whom and to it is all due. From time to time when friends thank me, I will tell them to thank Him a hundred times over. Pride is something that God says He hates and resists the proud, so I no way want to be in that crowd. All of our lives it took us to become what we are today. How can we expect God to change this overnight?

Before coming to Christ, He truly changed my life. I was Mr. Self Sufficiency; I didn't need anyone to help me in life, much less God! I worked all my life since I was six years old to get anything and everything I wanted to get. Even in the practices we began in our lives before Christ these things can be beneficial when we realize that He gave us the ability and health to do the better things in life. I began a discipline in my life of exercising and I didn't know it then, but He gave me the ability to do this very thing. Even with a pinched nerve and recurrent back problems, this went on for over 30 years of my life. This I know about pride is that it doesn't fall easy. We must continue to humble ourselves instead of allowing Pride to take us for a haughty fall.

In my beginning walk in Christ, His Spirit kept wooing me to go to the altar and humble myself and I obeyed every time. He asked this of me, caring not what anyone would think or say even to this day giving God all the Glory for the mighty work He did in my heart. He had good reason to take me down this journey because He knew all what I would be facing in my life to come. Later, I discovered that He had said something like this in His Word. PSALMS 95:1-2 Come and kneel down before the Lord our maker of Heaven and earth. He said for those that didn't that they would become heart hardened. When I first saw that I knew God was doing this for my good and again for His Glory. There was one time in about three years that I was questioning God: "Why me all the time?" God spoke to me and said that if I didn't go when I knew He was calling me that I could end up like 90% of the people in this church where I was attending. When I heard this I practically ran to the altar!

There was another reason for this call, or journey. God was having me listen in on the conversations of the appointed altar workers and I couldn't believe the things I was hearing which had nothing about really knowing and following Christ. God at this time spoke to me something I haven't forgotten to this day; He said that Satan will attempt to put into our thinking that we don't have the capability that God has given us, that God-given capability within us to minister to others in need.

Faith Adventures Episode 27
Sensitivity to Our Fleshly Sins- Brings Deliverance

One day, a coworker asked if we could go out and have a beer and I told him, as my conviction as a Christian, I will not drink. His response to me was that I was more of a Christian than the whole company put together (Flowers Baking Company). One other time, I was invited by another co-worker to a birthday party with heathens and I accepted. Isn't this what Jesus did and would still do today to reach the lost at all costs? Another much older co-worker religious man advised me not to go to this party and was trying to put condemnation on me if I did. I went and didn't drink anything offered to me and they never pressured me otherwise. I really had a chance to be a witness sharing His Word in this setting, so I'm glad I listened to the voice of God and not the other. This other co-worker still had a hard time with me accepting this invitation, even after I told him all that happened.

On another occasion I was on a bowling team with my co-workers and this particular night my whole team had not showed up. It was important for the leagues to play that night and the other team asked me to come alongside of them because someone that night had not showed up for their team either. This pressure came unexpectedly. They were talking about betting and when they approached me, they were trying to persuade me for just one dollar. In the quickness of the moment of the flesh, I agreed to gamble. I begin to think about more and more of what I just did and I didn't like it, so I took the matter to the Lord! I really don't believe I sinned because I was overwhelmed by the circumstances. When we are caught off guard not giving us time to react rightly, this is not sin according to God's Word. James

4:17 states Therefore to him that know to do good and doeth it not it is sin. This is not a practicing lifestyle of sin according to James 4:2-6. In 1 John 3:9 NIV No one who is born of God will continue to sin because God's seed remains in them; they cannot go on sinning, because they have been born of God.

That was the Holy Spirit doing what he has been functioned to do. That was a little nudge, but most believers today won't budge from their own ways. Let's remember the Bible says in Isaiah 55:8-11, "His ways are not our ways and our ways are not His." In fact, He said that His thoughts and ways are so much higher than any of ours. I was asking God to once again to intervene and get me out of the situation I had agreed to. Shortly, after I prayed, my whole team showed up! What a relief like a deliverance in the fact that my team never asked me to gamble or gambled themselves.

I believe most believers today think nothing of something like this, but God had put sensitivity in my heart towards anything that would be unpleasing in His Sight. When the Holy Spirit is nudging us in a manner of righteousness, we need to be listening and taking heed to the seriousness of the matter. Most believers today think nothing of these kinds of matters! We need to always see what God says about these matters and remain sensitive to the Holy Spirit's bidding. Too many of us listen to the flesh and do the betting or even worse. The enemy can use things from our past to condemn us now and for our future. He can be condemning us for our past sins, while we are reminding him of His eternal destiny. Our Adversary already knows where His destination is, and tries to drive us crazy reminding us of our sins. One of the first things the enemy does is to attempt to cause us to lose our real and new identity in Christ. We are constantly saying what we have heard and have been taught. The majority of the church cannot seem to come into a biblical mindset. We are constantly calling ourselves sinners or Gentiles and hearing these same things from our very leaders. According to the Epistles of the Bible, we were once sinners and the believers are addressed as saints or becoming saints. We don't need to receive his daily accusations because Christ has forgiven us of all of them. I realized because my identity was now in Christ, that I didn't have to take this nonsense. When we become His child and we are truly born again and walking in His Commandments and in His Spirit, we are pleasing in His sight. That means everything is alright in the vertical as well as the horizontal. This kind of relationship is God's desire for the believer that everything and everyone comes to reconciliation which forms the cross. This is when we can truly set our minds on the things above. We cannot set our life's ambitions into the cares and riches that can come from the attraction of earthly material possessions. Before I came to Christ, I had many women in my life looking for satisfaction for many years in my life. It wasn't until later I truly wanted a relationship by God's Spirit to walk in His Spirit and not to fulfill the lusts of the flesh.

When we have committed all we know to God, then we have received the revelation that our adversary the devil can only be an instrument in making us stronger in the Lord. We can beat him at his own game. It is because God's given wisdom has been imparted to us in understanding the strategies of the enemy, our adversary. The Scripture also says that when the enemy comes in like a flood, that the Lord will raise a standard against him. If we don't understand this, we can allow those thoughts to bring us into the entertaining of our temptations. Messiah Jesus said that we should pray that we not enter into temptation. When we are praying for a person or a situation, we cannot allow the enemy to get any place in our minds with stinking thinking. What the enemy brings into our mind about some girl or guy from the past, let's thank the devil for this, so that we can pray for this person. Through Christ and His word we can defeat the devil in his own tactics or the game he is trying to play in our minds.

Also, we must realize "Greater is he that is in you, than he that is in the world." This greatness comes to the Body of committed believers which together defeat principalities and powers in high places. We are no match for the devil within our own strength. Our strength comes through the Word of God and allows Him to change us in His power and methods in how He sees fit. He is all Powerful and when we realize it's His Power working through us, nothing can defeat us because nothing could defeat Him. Messiah Jesus needed the Word of the Living God which was and is the Spirit of prophecy to defeat the adversary! How much more do we need this daily in our life?

Let's make it a point to eternalize (memorize) 2Corinthians 10:5-6. My short version of this, that God gave me, is to cast it down and don't carry it around. (Fleshly thoughts) Too many of us are entertaining our minds with the things of the flesh, which is unpleasing to God and you will know it is sin when you have begun to talk yourself into it. This is exactly what happened to Eve in the garden. Here's is a shocking revelation: Just because we have thoughts of the most evilest things, doesn't necessarily mean that we have sinned. It's not the thought that gets lodged into our mind that is sin. The question is: What do we do with the thoughts that the accuser is throwing at us? God has said through the power and strength of His Word that we can cast every imagination down that is unpleasing to God.

If we are truly walking in His Spirit, what is unpleasing to Him should be unpleasing to us as His children. At some point in our life in Christ, His will must become our will and more and more will He grant you your desires, because they have become His desires! His desire is definitely not for us to live in sin, that is, making a practicing lifestyle of sin. According to what God says when we are truly born again we cannot practice living in sin! We have not been born again or we are a person in the state of being miserable beyond all men's comprehension. The Bible says 2 Peter 2:21 For it had been better for them not to of known the way of righteousness ,than after they have known it, to turn from the Holy Commandment delivered unto them. If we choose to continue to live in sin we have lost all sensitivity to God's Spirit. In my day when God would have me speak love but address sin, I would see many men and women turn away from their sins.

Faith Adventures Episode 28
God Given Job- God Kept Job

I have been working in Tampa for about four years' time for this baking company and a drastic change was happening. The bakery had been consistent in delivering our products to the agency before all the vendors would arrive. Things were changing at our agency and boy, could you hear everyone complaining. For some reason, they were not getting our products on time and this lasted for about two to three months. Many mornings we just sat around, waiting for our products and the men were not patient in their waiting stages. I have always been the positive type person that God made me after He changed me. I would always try to speak positive things into the most negative situations. This meant also we had to make arrangements to communicate to the head supervision at all of our retail stores.

Normally for receiving products they had a back-door receiver to check us in, but because of the time we were arriving that service was closed down. This made it more difficult to get our products checked in, so our waiting would become an issue with the majority of our vendors. It didn't with me because I would always carry my little Bible with me and meditate on it, while patiently waiting to get checked in. One day with the same dilemma, I was entering the store and the head supervisor wouldn't allow me to come in his store with the products. If this would have happened normally I wouldn't had said anything, but this was my last stop to drop off my products to finish up the day. I really blew it by getting upset with the situation and the supervisor that created this dilemma and called him some unwholesome name. He shouted to me "Don't you ever come into my store again". In this type of business, when you get thrown out of a store, it means you are unemployed. I went back into my step van and cried out to God, because I had nowhere else to turn. I prayed earnestly because I had a family and a responsibility to them and I didn't know what to do. I knew one man that was an ordained minister at this same time period that lost his job and wouldn't even bother to tell his family, this went on for over a year.

I was asking God to intervene in this situation, because I was at my wits end. It seemed to be the longest miles I ever traveled going back to the agency, not knowing what to expect. As soon as I arrived a good friend of mine approached me. He said to me: "My brother, you would not believe what happened here today." Then he said with his eyes wide open. "I saw it and I can't believe it happened!" Now he had my curiosity up. I asked him to tell me what happened that caused him to be so excited. I tried, but I could hardly get it out of him. I thought at the time, that I could use some good news about now.

He told me that our top supervisor when we were all present came out earlier and announced that Norman was no longer employed here. I remember he didn't like me because of my witness of Jesus Christ to him and others. As I remember he had put me in a very uncomfortable spot one time before to compromise. I was praying that God's will would be done concerning him in situations concerning dealing with him. Something no less than miraculous was about to happen and my brother told me that our immediate supervisor stood right up in front of him.

Our immediate supervisor told him that: "If you dismiss Norman, then you will have to dismiss me!" This was truly God's Intervention on my behalf. Not only did God do this, but God sent him back to his old job which was not a promotion, but a demotion. I can tell anyone especially believers without any reservations that if God has put you in a job or position, that He will keep you there until his timing is up for you to leave.

Faith Adventures Episode 29
Heathen Co-workers-Become God's Workers

God had many times through me, demonstrated His love to my co-workers and they saw God work on my behalf, but still they continued in their ungodly lifestyles. Practically every day they would mock God in one way or another. I knew God had sent me there amongst all these heathens to show the real love of Christ.

One day, I heard that one of my co-worker's wife and little girl had a bad accident that nearly took their lives. I believe God put on my heart to visit this family. I went to the hospital and no one was there but me and his family. The next day Bill, the father, in this family at work approached me. He asked me a question? What kind of Christian are you to go and visit and show love to my family, when all I ever do is mock you and your God? I responded that I believe everything the Bible says to do. The Bible tells me to love my enemies, though they won't receive the love of Christ in me. I showed love to their loved ones when they showed no love to me. Shortly after that, Bill began taking his family to church with him. He told me also how his mother was trying to smear my witness by telling him that she saw me entering into a bar. He told her that if he was in a bar it was a part of his route of serving bread. Being an example for Christ can go a long way with others.

There were two other co-workers that would occasionally get into conversations about how prejudiced they were regarding the black man. One day I was having a conversation with Richard, but I could see this was going nowhere, so I just decided to pray for him and avoid heated discussions. One morning I again overheard them in this same type of conversation. I approached them as the Spirit, I believe, led me to simply say. "If you say you love God and hate the black man, you do not have the love of the Father in you.". They didn't even hear it. Meanwhile, I had been praying about this whole situation. One day, maybe two years later, Richard, who was a minister also, was sharing with me how God showed him that he was prejudiced through some kind of situation in dealing with children. God had delivered him and used the seed of the Word of God and no doubt other things to bring him to see the light. I sat there listening, just being bountifully blessed within for the work God had done within my brother! I said nothing to take credit. I just began to give thanks and Glorify God for what He had done.

Some time, later I finished up rather late this particular day and I saw the bread distributor that was usually always gone long before we finished our work day. Tom came up and approached me and began to put his head on my shoulders and just weep like a baby of how wretched an alcoholic he was. When he was laying his head on me, I felt a little awkward, but immediately my thoughts were 'this was being like Jesus to Him in showing him, not just telling him about the love of the Father.' Shortly, he asked if he could come and attend my church? He came and God touched him and he told me so. What would've happened if I wouldn't have showed him Christ's love? I didn't allow my thoughts of what would they think of me if they saw this happening to take a hold of me.

My only transportation was a Honda 750cc motorcycle at this time. One morning the supervisor Joe approached me about my faith because I would regularly thank God for holding back the rain from getting wet on my ride to work. He said Norman, do you really believe that because you pray every day that God holds back the rain?

I do believe he does that for me in the morning when I ask, but not necessarily in the afternoon going home. Then I asked him if he knew about Elijah in the Bible? He answered of course not. I was sharing how Elijah prayed and it didn't rain for three years. He responded and said, "Norman please don't pray that way."

On another occasion, he approached me and said that if he could prove to me I gamble every day would I listen? I responded that every step I take is in the Lord and that's no gamble and walked away in disgust. Later in another Faith Adventure he also saw something miraculous happen to one of his loved ones.

About this same time period there was a woman vendor came to approach me then. She told me that she follows me. My curiosity was aroused. I said" What do you mean you follow me?" she said" I have watched you now for some time. My thoughts were what is this lady up to? This woman said "Every time you go in servicing your accounts it begins to rain and when you come outside and begin working getting your products together, I've noticed the rain actually stops. She was actually moved by my faith so much that she decided to follow my route pattern.

The revelation we must understand that it is God will get to His people in whatever manner He chooses. In conclusion, I would say that God can do a much better job of reaching people than any of us could ever imagine!

Faith Adventures Episode 30
Faith of a Little Child

During this same time that we were living in Tampa, we had some children gather in our home together to listen to Bible Stories on cassettes. I remember one little girl from our neighborhood in particular. After we gave her a Bible, she came by looking very sad one day because her dog had chewed up her Bible. Of course, we got her another Bible. She was a very beautiful little girl, and was some kind of a model even at the young age of seven years old.

Many children would come by, and sometimes even the older ones came. It was a joy to plant seeds of faith in their lives. One boy, James, came by on another day, and he asked me if I could take him to a soccer game because his dad, like many other dads, never had time for him. I told him that if he would ask permission from his dad, I would gladly take him. I really didn't care much for soccer, but it was all part of winning a little boy's heart to the Lord. In this same time period, one of my neighbors approached me and asked if I had told her little girl that Jesus loves her. I replied, "Yes, I did." She told me that she thought so, hearing about me as a neighbor. She also told me her daughter couldn't stop saying all day long that Jesus loved her. We will never know what that name will do unless we proclaim it!

James and I were heading to the stadium, and it was not looking to be a very good day. It was far from a clear day. As we approached the stadium, looking at the clouds, it surely looked like a big downpour was about to happen. My little friend began to get very disappointed, when he saw that this might ruin his very first time being able to go to a game, which he was looking forward to experiencing. I asked him if he remembered the Bible story of how Jesus calmed the storm. He said in excitement that he remembered this very story. I asked him, "Do you believe if we pray to the Father in Jesus' name that He could calm the storm today for you?"

He said without any hesitation "*I believe!*"

So as we were waiting in the line to get the tickets, we looked up. We could see the stormy clouds begin to separate, and we went in to see the game with just a few drops. That was what God did for a little boy who had the faith to believe! Today, the little boy is a man, and I think he will always remember what God did for him that day.

One of the older boys George came around quite frequently and at this same time I was missing some money. One day I confronted him of stealing and he denied his sin. I began to pray about this matter that God would reveal me something to know it was George. Another day he came back and as he entered the door he kissed me. Then I remembered how Judas kissed Jesus and betrayed Him. I once again boldly confronted him on this matter and he confessed he committed this act. I told him that I forgave him and he was amazed and he never came back again to visit.

Faith Adventures Episode 31
God's Favor in the Courts

At this time, my wife (ex-wife, now) and I had been married about four years. She of course missed her children and we decided to go to court to gain custody of them. We had to take a trip all the way to Maryland by taking off work for about two weeks. We were praying very much about this situation and asked many others to pray also. We had to meet with our lawyer and had to handle similar preliminaries.

Just before we entered the courtroom, we prayerfully decided to circle the courthouse seven times driving around the courthouse. This was like something that happened physically speaking in the Bible when God used men under Joshua. They marched around the city for seven days, and once on the seventh day seven times, and then through obedience to God they had the victory and the walls fell down and they overtook the city to go on to victory. We as believers can have the spiritual victory over the walls that keep us from the true blessings.

I can't remember too much about the court proceedings, but I do remember when they put me on the stand. They asked me to give a brief testimony of our living conditions. I mentioned being born again and the judge stopped me, and asked me to explain what I meant by becoming born again. This is what I would call a rare opportunity and I took it and didn't hold anything back!

They asked our son to whom did he choose to live with and my son told the judge that he would prefer to live with us. Our lawyer told us that things looked very bleak in how all this was coming down. I told him in response, and everyone else, that no matter what the decision was that these children were coming with us. I was standing on faith in accordance to how we prayed in accordance to faith.

We had to wait on the decision from the judge for some time, so we decided to head back home to get back to our daily routine, without the children and without any decision made at this point by the courts. My wife's faith was floundering day after day. I stood my ground in faith waiting in believing what we prayed! The decision from the courts finally came down. This was not what my wife wanted to hear. We had lost the court trial and the children were awarded to her ex-husband. Obviously, my wife was upset to say the least; I was there to comfort her in her distress for that day. I told her: "I don't care what the courts have decided. I don't know how but we will get these children in our custody. We must believe that which we prayed, that God would bring to pass the victory!"

Her ex-husband agreed to allow the children to come and stay with us for the summer. We even spent our time together having Christmas in July and that Christmas reminded me of the greatest movie I believe was ever put on the screen, "Christmas in Canaan.". Because of the costs of losing work and expenses for this entire court endeavor we had very little to give one another. This was one of my most favorite Christmas times because it wasn't about trying to out-give one another. We gave one another hand-me-down-clothes and that was it!

About this same time period we went to Circus World in Orlando and we had a wonderful time as a family. We were there all day and as we approached our car we took notice that it had been broken into and all my children's clothing and our belongings were gone. Sure, my family was disappointed and upset. On the way home, we stopped at a convenience store. Both my children saw something to give to and had a heart to give, what I was about to spend on them. This really touched God's heart and mine to seeing the unselfish response they demonstrated.

We decided to visit some friends as our last stop towards home. They asked us about how things were going and we naturally told them about our loss. They responded in love to us and gave my children more clothing than they had before and much better quality. It was things like this that encouraged us all that God was going to answer the prayer, the petition on behalf of our children! What God did was no less than miraculous. He subsequently granted custody of the children to us and they were with us for the remainder of the time.

Faith Adventures Episode 32
Debt Way Overdue-Paid in Full

Now we are going to step back briefly to my age of seventeen when I was working and accumulating money for my first motorcycle. At this time a friend of mine came to me in desperation to borrow $33.00 from me. I was reluctant in giving this to him because of my goal. He kept badgering me for it and assured me that he would give it back to me shortly. Later, I remember having to ask him for it on several occasions and it was a losing battle. Sometimes needing money can drive you to do the craziest things. I called him to have it out with him, not thinking this could have put me in quite a dilemma, if he would have taken me up on this. For many years for some reason, I couldn't get this out of my mind for ten years or more!

One day as a believer looking to grow and change to please my Heavenly Father I came across the Scripture that states: "And if ye do good to them which do good to you, what thank have ye? For sinners, also do even the same. And if ye lend to them of whom ye hope to receive, what thank have ye?" For sinners also lend to sinners, to receive as much again

Luke 6:32. The Scripture that God was having me zero in on by the power of the Holy Spirit, was that if I lend to them what I hope to receive? That's what I did as a Gentile and it got into my spirit mightily! I realized at this time I hadn't given to God this matter of still expecting a return. God knew what He was doing because He was preparing for me a greater revelation in coming to terms with this frustration. I gave this whole matter to God and told God I was going to try to look up my friend to tell him that I no longer in any way expected him to return this money. It was like the Lord speaks of as a deliverance that had occurred in my life.

When I went to visit him I actually found him and have not been able to even contact him, but once on the phone since then. When I told him, what God had done in me concerning this matter, he could hardly believe what I was saying to him. I know that this must have been a mighty testimony to him. He was all part of our gang that I grew up with. Like all my other friends I had been praying for him and by faith claimed his soul for the Kingdom also.

I believe there was another reason God brought this matter to the surface. The Bible says that when we have been faithful in the smaller matters, then God will give us greater matters. Today I can say that whatever Christ gives me as I have freely received I freely give, because He bought me with His purchased price and it's all His possessions now and all of my life I have given to Him! The Messiah has put such a love in my heart that I look for nothing in return, because it is He that is doing it through me. Let all that He has done, and will continue to do be for His Glory and His Glory Alone.

No wonder God is speaking to us in all generations, to be not only hearers, but become doers because that's when these truths become a revelation for you and many others for years to come. Becoming a doer takes time and He has our whole lifetime to speak to us. The Bible also tells us to do everything in word and deed in the Name of our Lord Jesus Christ. None of us start out being scholars, so we must humble ourselves to do what we understand to do by the Power of the Holy Spirit.

I remember when I first meditated on this Scripture I approached it in simplicity. My thought was that if I helped someone in some manner that I would try to remember to say to them, I did it all in the Name of my Lord and Savior Jesus Christ. I never had much ability with hands on things so I would stop when I would see someone broke down and get out my jumper cables and get them on their way. For many years, I put this into practice. One night about midnight while going to Bible College, I gave this man and his wife a jump and what happened six months later was unbelievable which you will read in the future Faith Adventures to come, God willing.

Faith Adventures Episode 33
Prayer of Faith Astounds the Doctors and the Courts

I'm still living in Tampa and in the early morning hours, my wife would take me to work. This particular morning right after she dropped me off, someone told me my wife has been in an accident just a few blocks down the street. I rushed out of the agency and I saw my wife's car and checked on her and my son and they were okay. The car had stopped right in front of a gas pump, so no doubt that was God's intervention. My wife at this time and I remember another time in Maryland had an accident in the Harbor Tunnel. When I asked her what she did she said she would just let go of the steering wheel and the car was under its own power to go wherever. After I checked on my wife and son, I saw the driver of the car that caused this whole incident. He was standing outside his car with blood trickling all over him after his head had been smashed into his windshield. This man was in severe pain and kept crying out about the glass that was in his eyes. I approached this man and asked if he would like me to pray with him before the ambulance arrived. Yes, he said with no hesitation. Even though he was in pain, he was seriously receiving this prayer of faith! God had me pray specifically that the doctors would be able to take every sliver of glass out of his eyes.

About two weeks later that man Bobby showed up at my home accompanied with his girlfriend. This man came by to thank me for praying for him. He told me that when he arrived at the hospital the doctors were discussing something very troubling to him in this dilemma. He overheard them speaking that this was going to be some kind of task of getting every sliver of glass out of his eyes. He told me he had remembered how God had me pray and that's why he was there to be thankful for what God had did.

I could see that he was talking in a redemptive manner. He was once again asking for prayer in the light of the charges he was yet to face in the courts. He was facing drunken driving, speeding and reckless driving charges. I prayed with him specifically that he would get nothing but court cost and for God to show Himself to this young man in about what God was about to do. I remember watching and hearing some of the final judgments that were coming down on others, much lighter sentences than usual by this judge. I overheard the lawyers saying that the judge for a change was in an unusually good mood today. When my friend went before the judge, facing all these charges the judge's decision was to give him a break and all he received was Court costs!

My friend and I knew this was God at work on behalf of my friend showing him God's goodness and love to him. What God had done with me for some time now was bring me to a maturity in praying for others. This is a good sign that we have matured in the Lord that we have come from that place of just praying for ourselves and our families, to the place in praying on others behalf. It has always amazed me how believers to this day will come to church asking us to pray for them and many times we will tell them that we will pray for them and many times never get around to it. Why don't we just step out in boldness like I have done many times and just pray for them right there? I have noticed most believers won't take it upon themselves to ask for prayer, even when prayer is offered by the pastor or otherwise!

Faith Adventures Episode 34
God Spoken Thanksgiving Through Faith

I have to take us back to how I handled sicknesses in my days before Christ. I would just go to work to work it off. I never missed a day of work because of sickness, because I was such a conscientious worker and didn't pay attention at all much in experiencing my pain. I had a pinched nerve and still exercised strenuously very often. Later, God touched and healed me in an upcoming Faith Adventure.

I am still living in Tampa and I was always a very conscientious worker. Once I had gotten so sick with the flu, with a 106 fever, that I could hardly stand up. I remember my wife trying to give me medications, but nothing was working. I began to pray in accordance to how I had learned many preachers at that time were preaching and teaching. I began to continually rebuke the devil. I was relentlessly praying in this manner and nothing was happening. All of a sudden in my silence God began to speak to me something very simple, but very profound. God was asking me: What did His son Messiah Jesus do? This was long before the fad of what would Jesus do in any situation would be said and believed.

I pondered on what God was speaking to me only to hear Him. He said Jesus only rebuked the devil or Satan one time. This was like God's Revelation imparted to me because I was a believer to always look and hear what God said about any matter. It came to me that day, probably for the first time, the Revelation of Faith. After all, I remembered the Scripture says that we cannot please God without faith. I believed what God was saying to me, more than what many preachers were saying and at that time I heard them all. He was beginning to put a faith in me that I never heard of before. My response was that I just kept thanking Messiah Jesus for what I had asked and believed I would receive. The very next day, I was back to work and feeling fine.

Some time, after this, God had me meditate on John 15:7. He says that if we abide in Him and He abides in us that we can ask whatever we will and we will receive. Abiding in Him is the condition and this means commitment, nothing less than totally trusting Him and putting your whole life in His Hands in obeying Him. As I have presented this prayer many times, I realize sometimes these things take time. Rarely does He do things instantly. It is our attitude that He is looking upon while we are experiencing the sickness. If we look at sickness as a positive thing, we understand these fluids have to empty out of our system so let nature takes its course. Meanwhile just believe what He says and meet His conditions; it will be over before you know it!

Remember faith is the key ingredient to continue to believe. Don't keep asking, but if we really believe He has heard us, just keep thanking Him for your healing or anything we ask in accordance to His will. This is why I believe that God had me title this book "Faith Adventures." My greatest adventures are attributed to hearing God on all matters!

Faith Adventures Episode 35
Faith through Prayer-God's Supernatural Method.

I'm still in Tampa and living in a trailer park. One day my stepson came rushing into our home with our neighbor accompanying him. I could see she was really upset with the fact my son was up in a tree and was screaming, and she had seen that he had poisonous caterpillars crawling all over his arms. By the time they entered the home you could see the welts up and down his arms. Our neighbor just happened to be a nurse and was urging us to take our son to the Emergency room immediately!

My pastor was visiting that very day and we were fellowshipping at this time. I told the nurse that since my pastor is here that we were first going to take this matter to God. I believe she left frustrated, thinking we were probably crazy and we began to pray. Normally, when I pray, I pray with my eyes completely closed and this time was different. For some reason I had my eyes open just before the prayer ended and had never seen anything like this in my whole life! I saw an instantaneous miracle right before my eyes for the first time. I actually saw the welts disappear right before my eyes! I was thanking God and rejoicing for what God had just done.

Another time in my life in the same time period, I was visiting some very close friends at Daytona Beach, Florida. I believe I was just sitting there reading the Bible or some good book, just relaxing. All of a sudden two teenage boys came barreling into the living room really frantic and frightened! They had just come from the beach and they said a man of war had bitten both of them and they were in terrible pain and discomfort. I saw the parent's reaction which was also frantic, looking for information in books of what to do? They were trying other methods and considering taking them to the Emergency room. I was trying to speak above all the excitement, and the noise, to suggest that we pray. They didn't seem to pay attention much to what I was saying. I just boldly begin to pray, not knowing rather they heard me or were even paying attention to me. That's something I have experienced many times before with many believers; they always seem to resort to other methods first.

I knew God heard me and had the confidence in what He would do on behalf of my friends. One boy was a close friend to the other who lived at the home we were visiting. The friend that was visiting began to see the bruise from the bite disappear and he was not a believer. I told him this is God's love being demonstrated to you, that you might believe on Him for yourself. The son of the household believed God was at work and within the break of the day; his bruise from the bite had completely disappeared also.

Why do we, when we are faced with situations like this, seem to first resort to doctors and other men's methods? He has said in His Word to cast every care upon Him because He Is a God that cares much. It reminded me of a lady a non believer, showing her the Bible regarding in praying for her child and she believed and received in an upcoming Faith Adventure.

If you right away don't see results, then take other measures. I've known believers to pray in faith along the way to the doctors or emergency room situations, and things that did appear or symptoms would change right along the way or, as they would be walking through the doors. Many times, the doctor, after examining the patient, would ask them, "Why did they bring them there?" This is when we have the opportunity to give God the Glory when these things happen caring not who hears it or who is around!

Faith Adventures Episode 36
God Given Faith to Reach the Children

My job in Tampa was to service many grocery stores with daily bread. This gave me the opportunity to meet many children. I used to say all the time that I give out the Bread of Life in Jesus Christ. I had great joy in what I believe God had placed me into doing. They all knew me because of His witness put within me to proclaim Him day after day in some way or another. Many children would gather around my truck after they got out of school. They love me telling them the stories of the Bible!

One day, one of the fathers of the children came in the store and confronted me in his anger. He said that I heard you have been talking to my child about the Lord? I never denied this and told him that I had talked to many of the children about the Bible. I don't think he was ready for my response. I told him that I was so glad to meet him. I also told him that I was so glad you came to talk to me about this matter, because I would also like to talk to you regarding your soul. He turned away from me and literally ran out the door! The fruit of this was marvelous, because we ended up taking his son to church for a short time. So the seed was planted in that young man's life in a powerful way.

About this same time God had me ministering to a gal that just began to move in with her boyfriend. When she heard what God had to say on this matter, she was convicted and she moved immediately out of this beginning to be sinning lifestyle!

One evening, I was watching this man on Christian television telling how he was reaching young children for Christ by just sharing His love and His Word. As I was praying about this matter, God put it on my heart to just go to the schools, and just walk and talk with these young ones. At this age they were really listening and receiving. I couldn't tell you how many different schools I had went to. I can only tell the things I remember. One day as I was talking to them, more and more came around me. I shall never forget that I was in the circle of a crowd of twenty or thirty young teens and they were captive to everything God said through me to them.

As I was walking away, God completely by His Spirit came upon me and I was humbled, and I walked away weeping in an indescribable joy. I had never experienced anything like this in my entire life and it caused me to keep doing this. God had me also give out some Bibles and I would write my name and phone number in these Bibles. About a year later, I received a call from a young man and I was so blessed to receive such a call. He wanted to talk to me and ask me how God felt about sexual impurity. God had me minister to him about this thing that has destroyed millions. I believe he received what God said and is walking in it today. We can never measure the fruits by what we see happening, but by faith, knowing God is doing something in the hearts of men and women. God says that if we do our part, how so much more will He do His part in accordance to His Word!

His Word says in Isaiah 55:8-11, even as natural as the rain and snow fall from Heaven as the same way this affects our earth. His Word will not go out void, but it will do what He sent it out forth to do. When it's His Word, it is Mighty and alive to awaken those from death. His Word shall surely accomplish what He said if we have Faith.

Later, after I began attending Bible College, God put it on my heart to do this same very thing in Colorado Springs, Colorado. One morning I was walking with this gal and I hadn't usually done this, but I put my arm around her to show her the Father's love. Later that day I was at my brother's home and he told me that he had been trying to contact me. He said, "Norman you are in big trouble for going to that school today." God willing, you will find out what happened in the upcoming Faith Adventures.

Faith Adventures Episode 37
Faith Tested-Outcome Miraculous

A lot of times God does things simultaneously to begin to demonstrate a truth in accordance to the Scriptures. The Scripture I am referring to is 1 Timothy 4:11, 13, 15 and 16 NASB. These things the Lord says to command and teach. We are to be an example as a believer in word, in conversation in love and to live out a life of purity. God is also saying to be attentive to what is said in accordance to sound doctrine, and to meditate on these things giving our whole being to them. That which God is saying beforehand is prior to a promise God has given to those that would have the revelation from God to receive this bountiful truth by faith.

In verse 16 it states: "Take heed unto thyself and unto the doctrine; continue in them: for in doing this thou will both save thyself and them that hear thee." Just about in any translation you will discover this same truth. Pay close attention to yourself and your teaching; persevere in these things, for as you do this, you will ensure salvation both for yourself and for those that hear you. This is a promise for those that will be willing to live in a life of obedience. I have seen the fulfillment of this Word many times, so many that I cannot possibly count them. Yes I do believe in a name it and a claim it Gospel. God has put this faith in my heart to have a God driven walk for souls to be in the Kingdom of God.

Again God gave me this Scripture. I was beginning to believe this awesome truth, and it just seemed so simple that I think many have overlooked this and the power that is entailed in this. I was about to have a test of faith to see whether I really believed what this was saying. The enemy did not want me to see the reality of this truth, so he brought into my path one of the most hopeless cases, which practically everyone else wouldn't bother to even take the time to talk to.

This man's name was Herman and when I met him, I could see that he was a bit physically challenged and a lot of people that met him would say he was mentally challenged as well. Let's just say this; he is not one that you would invite to your daughter's birthday party! This man, when he came to church he would look over the women with a lustful evil eye. He would also even cut himself up usually in his wrists during the service, but yet he professed to know Christ. You can understand why believers thought of him as a very hopeless case and were afraid of him. He was even trying to pursue my own wife and at one point, I shoved him on the church property, but never bodily harmed him. For some reason that I couldn't figure out, this man followed me around like a puppy dog, but I would watch him as if he was a Doberman Pincher.

Now you can see how I was being tested about this Word Revelation that I was receiving. One day outside the church, this man was standing out in the middle of the traffic daring people to hit him. I had heard he had done this on many occasions. He walked up to me after making such a display for all to see. I told him that you are not going to kill yourself. He looked at me and responded, "How would I have said such a thing?" I simply told him that I have claimed your soul for the Kingdom of God. At this point he, along with others, thought I was crazier than him.

I just simply believed God would do what He said He would do in accordance to His Word. If we are to do our part in believing in faith, God will do exceedingly abundantly above all we ask Him to do, especially when He has given us the heart to do this. I was being tested and tried to the fullest extent that a man could stand.

I will briefly tell this part about Herman. I left Tampa to go to Bible College in Colorado for four years and left Herman in God's Hands. I remember he said to not forget to pray for him. I never heard or seen anything of him for five years. He showed up later on my church steps and he told me he was a truly changed man, and I will talk about this in the future Faith Adventures, God willing.

Faith Adventures Episode 38
Continuing to Be His Witness-Despite My Greatest Trial

According to Philippians 4:10, Paul had learned to be content in whatever circumstances he faced. According to Thayer's Lexicon, learning means to increase one's knowledge to obtain the knowledge of Christ. It also means to learn by use of practice by being accustomed to make a habit of such things. We must remember what the Lord said to Ananias in a vision that he and Paul experienced in Acts 9:16, God said that he would show him how much he would suffer for His sake. This was the cross that Paul had to endure. I will be speaking of the cross I have had to endure also.

God will not deal with most of us in the same manner. When we experience different circumstances in life, like having very little, we should rejoice and be thankful that we are there. This is all part of God's learning plan and His process in humbling us. This will take time and patience, depending on the cross He has designed for us in our lives. If we remain obedient in these times, they can become another avenue to full contentment. Many of these times I have experienced and I have learned to draw more to Him. Proverbs 3:5 and 6 (NASB) states, "Trust in the Lord with all your heart, and do not lean on your own understanding. In all your ways acknowledge Him and He will make your paths straight." Many of us have memorized this verse, but have we eternalized it into our life every day? Have we come to the place to serve Him unconditionally? Could we say without reservation that we would continue to serve Him, if we received nothing from Him for our remaining days? This is the journey of contentment that God desires for all of us. It is being dependent on Him in everything that He does; I know is for my good.

This episode is something I don't like writing as much as the others. I'm still in Tampa working as a Vendor and being the witness that God has called me to be. My wife had become or was looking to become unfaithful in our marriage. I knew this because one night she gave me an ultimatum. She was giving me a hard choice, in fact the hardest choice, I've had to make up to this point in all my life. She simply said to me very seriously, that it was either going to be me or this Jesus. I told her that if I would choose you over the Lord of my life, I believe I would be a hypocrite in God's eyes. That's the last thing I would do, but if it means losing you, so be it.

The very next day the whole atmosphere of my home had changed. I sat down to relax to turn on the TV and there was no TV and a lot of others things she took, including the fish aquarium and all our fish. I began praying, not quite understanding what just had happened to me. I cried out to God, "Why me, what did I do to deserve this?" I know I needed a lot of changing that God had yet to perform in me, but still couldn't understand why. I have always ended my prayer in this manner, no matter what I have had to go through. No matter what Lord, I'm still going to serve You.

The very next morning, I opened my Bible and I could see where my departed wife was spiritually. In accordance to 1 Corinthians 11, this talks about how the man is the covering over the wife, with of course the man under submission of the Head, being Messiah Jesus. She had lost her covering and couldn't even pray again in accordance to the Scriptures. At this time I couldn't say it was a joy to go to work because of all the people I would have conversations with, they would probably ask about my wife. I would always talk about my wife and the fact that we were happily married, especially when

I had conversations with the opposite sex. This was the last thing I was looking forward to that day, and really didn't want to go to work. I prayed and told the Lord, "I will continue to be your witness on my job. I will trust You will continue doing in and through me what you choose to do." I died as to how I felt or even thought about this whole dilemma.

This was most definitely, the hardest day I had ever faced in my whole entire life.

I was praying that no one would ask me anything about my wife or family, because she also took her two children. God was faithful and answered my prayer and no one asked me anything that first day. It has now been two weeks and I never had heard anything of their whereabouts. I couldn't sleep for the whole two weeks and was so worrisome of what had happened to my family. I asked some believers at my church and no one seem to want to tell me what happened. Instead I was blamed by practically the whole church because of the zeal God had put in me.

There was one true brother that seemed to have a good idea of where they were. He told me that she was with another man, a Jewish man, not even a Christian. He just professed to be one and was able to persuade her to live with him and gave her practically nothing. The fact that he was Jewish had nothing to do with what had happened in my eyes.

I found out where he lived and drove over there one night to see if this was true. I saw my wife's car in his parking lot space, and then I knew it was true. At first, I was thinking about making a big scene in the middle of the night and didn't know what I would have done if I would have listened to my flesh. I was praying earnestly and went home and had some relief of the fact that I knew where she and the children were now. In this two- week period of time I had developed a cyst on my neck and it was getting worse. I didn't care about that, but my friends in Daytona did and said I was going to their doctor to have it lanced. When I had that done, I felt hardly any pain, because of so much pain going on inside of me at this time. I never in that whole period by the grace of God went to their home to make trouble or even speak to them.

One day about six months later, I was in the store working, and for the first time I saw them together. This was too much for me to bear, so I went to the back of the store asking God what He would have me do? I know I did what He wanted me to do, because if it had been up to me, I would have bashed his face in. I followed them out to the car and was pleading with my wife to come home, that I have forgiven her, but she gave me nothing but the answer no.

I approached him and preached some judgment on him instead of sending him into judgment! He had a rather huge friend with him a lot I found out later. This man knew all about the situation and when he saw me approach my wife's adulterer and heard what I said to him, he commented that he liked me. So, no doubt I was a witness to his friend also, doing what God wanted me to do, not what I wanted.

There was one point my wife came to visit me asking about whether I had signed the divorce papers, which was something I put off for some time, believing God was going to do something. There was another time that she asked me to use my insurance at work to help her with some operation. I was shocked that she would even ask me something like this, because this man owned several homes and many other material things. I told her that this man does not love you, because he doesn't show it.

I took this matter to prayer to God like I do all matters. God told me to do this; to show His love through me to her, even though she didn't deserve it. This matter went on for about two years, believing

God was going to bring her back to me. God had given me more than enough faith to believe and even this He can do!

In this same time frame I went to a meeting and a known lady minister shared from Book of Ecclesiastes that God would lose a woman from a man because of the bonds of her wickedness. God spoke to me something that I shall never forget. He said it was easier for me to move Pikes Peak Mountain, than it was to move her will. This word I heard from the Lord was a sure word. I gave the matter to God completely!

I will touch on this much more in the coming Faith Adventures of how God spoke to me a promise and I held on to that promise for eleven years. I know today that God doesn't necessarily put together everyone that are Christians. We must wait on God for the one that God has specially chosen and handpicked for us.

This was overwhelming, as a believer, I couldn't understand why my first wife left me for another man and wanted a divorce. I couldn't quite grasp that Jesus understood and had experienced the same thing. Then I came to the acceptance of His Word and believed it, though I didn't understand at the time. The Word spoken to me at this time was Hebrews 2:17 -18. He said that He had to be made like us in all things. He was tested in all things and was able to aid us in our tests. God, in my pain, spoke to me and said: Throughout times and times My people have been rejecting and divorcing Me. This was a clear spiritual revelation of the picture of the Body of Christ today.

We must learn to approach the Word of God always as a child. A little child may ask today; where did God come from or how did He come to be? Our answer should always be in accordance to the Scriptures. God has always been from the beginning and will be for all eternity. According to 1 Kings 8.56, not one Word of His promise according to all He promised would fail. Once we have grasped the

Truth that whatever God says is infallible, then we are well at the place that God would have us to be!

Humbleness and pride are as different as day and night. I have yet, to find anything good about pride in the Bible. In fact, I have discovered the exact opposite. God speaks of pride unceasingly as something that He resists.

There are many references to God hating pride. He refers to it as the pride of life, rebellious in nature, arrogance of heart, contentious, and these lead to perversion. Pride was always found in the nations that fought against Israel's land and people. According to Thayer's Lexicon (1 John 2:16) "Pride of life is an insolent and an empty assurance, which trusts in its own power and resources. It shamefully despises and violates divine laws and human rights. An empty presumption, which trusts in the stability of earthly things, displayed in one's lifestyle." Pride can lead us into self- destruction. Pride can cause us to trust in man's power and resources. According to Psalms 36:11, David spoke let not the foot of pride come upon me. According to the Theological O.T. Wordbook, "Foot means that the main force of word throughout the O. T. is the individual's feet are mentioned as traveling or holding dominion, like a beast."

I believe this is saying that we should not allow pride to take a step into our lives and to step forward into humbleness. God would say to us, don't allow pride to take place in your life!

Faith Adventures Episode 39
To Have Faith When No Faith in Sight

This was a time in my life that was the hardest to endure because this is something for any man or woman only God can get us through! My wife had just departed for the last time. At this time, I was putting my whole heart into ministry that I knew to do. It just seemed like that no one wanted to be neither mentored or become a disciple. So, I had nothing to reflect back to of what God had done through me. I was to the point of near depression and I heard my Heavenly Father say simply, Remember Noah. Noah didn't have anyone to come into the Ark, because no one was listening. I felt very strongly the same way. I thought, what do I have to show for all my efforts? As a new believer, I think I had a right to be discouraged, when nothing seemed to be happening because of His service through me to others. I didn't really understand the faith He had put within me at this time.

When God speaks something to us by His voice, we need to take heed and listen and allow Him to change us, not allowing the circumstances all around us to change us. Then I was reminded of my brother Gary and how God had used me to bring him back on the path with God. God by His Spirit had me ministering to him about holiness in cleaning up his act. I knew this was God speaking into my brother's life because he later became a minister and pastored churches in the Tampa Bay Area. We were a pair that was on fire for God and I had the honor of mentoring this man of God for years and came to love his wife and children very dearly. We had fellowship with God I couldn't count the times. We saw God answering our prayers in miraculous ways and we believed God could do anything! We even from time to time preached together!

On my job I met many believers but very few which I would consider believers that are serious about His Word and the things of God. At this particular restaurant where my two brothers were employed, I serviced them with bread several times a week. The owner and manager which was a believer also told me something one day that was very encouraging. He told me that before you come in our establishment, there is like a worldly atmosphere in this place. This is because of the continual conversations that are less than uplifting. When you come in, you are always speaking about the things of God and I know I can always count on you to bring encouragement. When you leave, the whole atmosphere changes in this place!

One evening I invited two natural born brothers of the faith who worked at this restaurant to my home. When they first arrived, I was preparing something for them to eat. The Bible does teach that we are to treat the brethren with a greater love than others. As I was serving them just simply some sandwiches, they seem to be so thankful as if my current wife had fixed them something very special. They commented to me in serving Christ that no one in their circles of Christianity had ever showed them this kind of love. We continued in fellowshipping, talking about the great things God was doing. At one point the younger brother and young in the Lord also was asking me about a matter. He shared with me how he had been trained in martial arts for some time now and had achieved a black belt in Karate. He was sharing with me of how he felt like the Lord didn't want him doing this anymore.

I'm not here to argue about rather this is right or wrong but the fact the Holy Spirit was ministering to him about this matter made it wrong for him. I began to share Psalms 91 with him and the power of God's Word written within the Scriptures. He received Psalms 91 very well and took it upon himself to memorize and eternalize this Psalm. He told me on a later date that he was telling his master trainer that he was going to quit and he got extremely upset telling him that because he trained him to the point he told him he owned him. I told him to get Psalms 91 into your spirit and God will show you His Power. He told me that one night his instructor called and this brother only opened up the Psalm and his former to be no more instructor hung up and never called back again.

Less than two years later, I received a call from his mother that he was killed in a car accident.

What a shock to hear such news about a brother and friend dying at such a young age. His mother apologized that she hadn't contacted me until after this incident, but she knew God had used me to put a persevering faith within her son. She told me that it is as if he knew, he was going to die soon and he asked the family before the accident to read Psalms 91 at his funeral processions. I could hardly believe what I was hearing. She then told me that he had copied this Psalm and it was everywhere in the house, so I know he truly got this Psalm in his spirit. This is a powerful example of how God's Word would not come back void and shall accomplish that which God sent it to do found in Isaiah 55:11. I have no doubt at all this Psalm made an impact on his family and friends because of the impact it had on this one young man's life. I know without a shadow of a doubt that he is in the Kingdom of God being absent from the body and being present with the Lord in God's mighty Presence!

Faith Adventures Episode 40
Bahamas Cruise Gift Given in Pure Love

I'm still in Tampa working and at this time my wife had already left me for another man. Just before this, I was endeavoring to win a bread contest, so that we could both go on a Bahamas Cruise. This seemed to be my last chance in showing my wife love. When we were told about the contest, I told my supervisor and co-workers that I was going to win. My co-workers looked at me like I was crazy and said some other things. My supervisor spoke up and said to us all: If Norman says he is going to win this contest, I'm telling you right now he will win and will do it honestly.

I had spent many evenings asking people in the stores to please try my product and many did. Sometimes I would stay in the stores until they nearly closed. I remember one day I was just finishing up my delivery that day and a woman frantically approached me. I had just told her little girl, like I have thousands of times that Jesus loves her. The lady said to me: You are the one! I thought, what have I done now? She was excited in what she was about to tell me what had happened concerning all of her family. She was telling me how her and her husband came out of Jehovah's Witnesses. She began to tell me how her father and the other relatives came out also. She also told me they were attending the same Baptist church that we had attended when we first came to Tampa. I still haven't figured how that would have come about, but she seemed very happy. I asked the Lord, what did I say or do that brought this about? God said to me, this is all that you told her John 14:6 "I Am the Way the Truth and the Life." That's the power of His Word with the faith He has given me to claim souls for the Kingdom!

The guys at the agency began to accuse me of doing something wrong in breaking the rules concerning the bread contest. I told them I did it in complete honesty, but they still didn't believe me. My supervisor did, and God was my witness and that was enough for me. I had heard some others had broken the rules to try to win, but I said nothing to anyone about this. In this same time period one of the salesman while turning in his money, noticed there was a Scripture on the bill. The first thing they did was blame me for this, which was ridiculous. I told someone the Scripture says: It's better to be buffeted for good than evil. Now I had won this contest for a vacation for two all-expenses paid!

My wife had left me in this time of my life which I mentioned in the prior Faith Adventure. At this point, I wasn't very much excited about going on a cruise. At this same time period, I was thinking about this special family in Daytona. During this time, they had allowed me to come over many times to have fellowship with them through this most trying time in my life. The Lord had reminded me of a conversation we had concerning their marriage and the tough times. Most importantly, I remembered them telling me that they could not afford to go on a honeymoon. So they never had time after ten years of marriage to go on one. I asked them would they be able to take the time now, ten years later and they said that they would. I told them that I had won a contest for two to go on a cruise, and if they would like to go on that honeymoon they missed? They could hardly believe this was happening, and excitedly said they would love to!

I told them I had to make the arrangements for this to be possible. I'm back to work and the time is coming near for me to go. Several of my co-workers asked me when I was going on this trip. I told them that I wasn't and boy, did that get some minds whirling. The questioning went on: What do you mean, by your not going because we know you won the contest?

This is when I told them I gave it away, to a special couple that never had a honeymoon. They just couldn't believe even a Christian, would do such a thing after working so hard to win the contest. Some of my close friends as believers understood this was God's love demonstrated through me to others. It was because God spoke it into my heart to do so. Sure, I had thoughts of the fact I could take just about any girl on a trip like this. In that era of time Bahamas cruises costs $3,000.00 or more. They were so thankful and I was completely thankful for what God had me do, despite all the gestures from many.

This same couple has blessed us in so many ways to this day that I can't begin to tell you the expression of the hospitality gifting of giving to them which has been directed our way and into many others lives.

When we stay sensitive to God's Holy Spirit in obedience, we can't even imagine what the outcome will be later. Preachers speak about a hundred or a thousand-fold. This is the way to sow seed with pure love in expecting nothing in return.

We have received so much more than that. In the future Faith Adventures, God willing, you will hear of more than the miraculous that God has done to this day. All I can do along with my family is give Glory to God and Alone to Him be given the honor, the praise and the Glory for what He has done!

Faith Adventures Episode 41
God's Miraculous Healing Power-Baby

The setting is that I'm still in Tampa Florida and doing my route day after day. One of my last stops which I served earlier than usual was a small business meat market. I was limited in this store with the items I sold, so I usually didn't spend much time there. One day, I saw that this Spanish lady was working the cashier. I also took notice that she was really upset about something. Recently she had a baby and of course everyone was rejoicing about this. This day, about a month after the baby was born, she told me the baby had a brain stem condition of cancer. I felt the Compassion of Jesus just welling up within me and I was taking a step of faith like no other time because I believed every Word the Bible taught. I opened my Bible and I had her read this passage. I asked her: "Do you believe God can touch your baby if we pray?" She said with a resounding: "Yes!"

We prayed together in agreement in accordance to Matthew 18:19-20 Jesus said: "Again I say unto you, That, if two of you shall agree on earth as touching anything that they shall ask, it shall be done for them of my Father which is in heaven."

Jesus said that He did the miracles that they may believe on Him. So, you might say I could have been putting myself in an embarrassing situation, but in reality, I was putting God on the spot. I have learned that He likes to be put on the spot, so that He alone may get the Glory! So we prayed together believing God together. God was showing me that He wanted me to step out in faith more and more as I matured in Him.

I came in the store and I saw her husband and he had brought the baby to the store. I don't believe it was a coincidence that I came right at that time. I have to admit I was a bit nervous in asking, if this was her baby that was in the hospital. She said yes, isn't it wonderful that God healed my baby. Since this was one of the first times I took a step of faith like this, I wasn't sure what had happened until she told me. I was completely amazed at what God had done. It was so miraculous; I could hardly believe what I was hearing and even seeing.

A few days later I could see this lady was upset again. She told me the doctor's report came back and the cancer had returned. I simply said to her that you know what God did and he will continue to do if you continue to believe. She listened and believed to the Jesus within me speaking to her and the baby was completely healed a few days later.

God was showing me also that by believing in Him, there is nothing impossible for Him to do and there is no such thing as coincidences but God- incidences. At this time, God was doing things with the people I knew on my route that were no less than miraculous. There was one young lady and she just began to move in with this man and I shared with her how God felt about that. She immediately got out of that situation that she now knew was unpleasing to God. I never shall forget what my supervisor said about what he knew I was doing practically every day. He said to me something so profound, I never have forgotten it. He said: "When you go out there and do what God has you to do, Norman, you cause people to look at the other side of themselves and in a lot of cases they won't like that."

In this same time period, Fred and I became friends. One day, I asked if he could help me with some repairs needed to done at my mobile home. We had to tear off the tin of the trailer to get to the problem. When we opened the tin there were hundreds of fiery red ants that had made a nest there. I went to get my bug spray and began spraying them and I didn't notice, but they were falling and crawling all over my arms. Fred saw this and asked, "Aren't those ants biting you?" I responded, knowing the Spirit of the Lord was upon me. "They can't bite a child of God," and then began with no fear flicking them off my arms one by one. Normally because of fear I would have panicked and went bananas. I had been bitten prior to this time by these same species and I hurt for weeks. I heard later that ants can sense whether you have fear or not. This was probably done to be a witness to this man what it can mean to have a personal relationship with Jesus Christ.

Faith Adventures Episode 42
Testimony to My Supervisor-God's Miraculous Healing Power

The setting: I'm still in Tampa working for Flowers Baking company. I don't remember how I met the supervisor's dad, Francis, but I must have been talking to him about salvation and he was considering going to church. I believe the whole family was Catholic. It was on a Sunday morning that I left by myself to go pick up Francis.

At this time in my life I had a habit of picking up hitchhikers, and there were nights when I just plainly went out to find them, that was what I believe at that time God was putting on my heart to do. I remember picking up one man that had a pole in his hand and threatened to hit me with it. I told him that I was not afraid of him and that God would take care of me because He had me on a mission of picking up hitchhikers. I never heard of any such ministry, but I was and still in love with Jesus today and I wanted to share my faith with almost anyone. One time, a man told me he was going to Orlando so I told him; we're going to go to Orlando. He was ready to listen to anything being thankful for the ride. I once heard in college that we can preach just about anything to the sinner, if we are showing him love and he knows it's love. Just before I dropped him off he asked me: "Why did you do this for me?"

I responded: "Because Jesus told us to go the extra mile for others and I'm just doing what Jesus would say for us to do." As a young believer, I never much tried to figure out things theologically, but just simply doing what God has said to do, and I believe that is the best theology we can learn. Someone once said that it's much better to be a fool for Christ than a scholar on ice.

So again, I'm on my way to pick up Francis for church, and I see a hitchhiker on Sunday morning, which was very rare. He climbed in the car and began cursing, and had some cocaine to snort and was putting it right up in front of my nose. I said: "No thank you, I no longer do those things because I get my high all the time off Jesus."

Then he said two things I wasn't ready for. First he said he was a Jew and I told him that I really respect the Jewish people because of their love for God. He then asked me where we were going. I told him that I'm on my way to pick up this man to take him to church. He then said something that really shocked me: "Then that's where I am going" and of course, I agreed to take him even in his state of mind. We picked up my new friend in Christ, and we were heading back in the same direction and stopped at the light that I had picked up this Jewish man. The Jewish man opened his door and was getting out. I asked him: "Did you change your mind about going?" He said: "I really believe you would take me." It was like the devil was driving him out quickly for this trip.

He may have been testing me, but I really don't know for sure, but one thing he knew for sure and found out; I was sincere and meant business. Somehow I believe as life goes on with these and others, God will or has shown Himself to them and no doubt will continue to do so. This same older man Francis, that I took to church, had called me to visit with him in the hospital. The first thing he told me was that gangrene had become a part of his foot and they were talking about amputating it. I told him that our Lord and Savior Jesus Christ could heal him like He did many other people in the Bible. We prayed together in accordance to God's Word joined with others as the Body of Christ believing God for a miracle. A week later, I walked in and this old man had the biggest smile on his face from ear to ear. He told me that the gangrene had miraculously healed up and his foot would not be amputated. Glory to God then and now. It wasn't much longer after that, that He went into God's presence "absent from the body is to be present with the LORD." The main thing was that he was ready and God used all these things to make it possible for him to be in God's Kingdom.

Faith Adventures Episode 43
God's Miraculous Multiplication

The setting is still in Tampa, waiting to go on a month's vacation, renting a vehicle to drive to Colorado Springs and the west coast. I have now received a month's pay, which half of it I was awarded as part of the vacation from the Bahamas prize. It was just days before I was to leave and God began to speak to me about giving Him His part of tithes before I left on this vacation. This was quite a test and I was trying to rationalize things in my mind, but the bottom line is that I gave all that He asked in obedience. This obviously gave me less for my vacation than I had anticipated, however I knew as He always has and always would stretch my dollars.

I always gave to God in obedience to Him, His tithes and offerings and whatever else that He would ask of me. One thing God has never done and that was to ask more than I had to give. He always knew what I had and prompted me by His Holy Spirit, in how and who to give to, but the tithes were a given.

I was seeing God's creation in a marvelous way. This was the first time I saw mountains on the west coast. I don't know why I went out there except to see God's creation in a different way and of course just to get away and be alone with God because of the crisis I was facing presently.

I had the desire to go to a Mega Nazarene Church in Denver, to meet the man that wrote the discipleship program that made a powerful change in our church in Tampa. I don't know why, but I was like in the balcony area and he came up and introduced himself to me. I told him how much his discipleship program was an instrument with prayer in changing our church to bring us into Revival. He seemed to be interested about what was happening with me. I told him about what I was going through and I remember him saying to me of how tough that must be. I could see it in his eyes that he began to develop a burden for me and he wasn't even my pastor. I told him that by God's strength He will see me through.

I never thought about it until now, but I wouldn't be a bit surprised that he didn't ask his church members full of disciples to pray for me. God can have people praying for us that we don't even know, and that truly is imparted by God's Holy Spirit prompting them to do so. We all need to be more faithful in what and who God is having us pray about by the prompting of His Holy Spirit. How can we be faithful and fruitful in our lives for others if we haven't allowed the Holy Spirit to have His way in our lives to come into a life of obedience?

This was also a chance for me to be a witness to people I never met or seen before. I've always said as long as there are people, there will always be something to do or be to them to show them for the first time in their life the love of Christ, and that's the way it should be. I remember traveling south slowly because I was in no hurry to get anywhere. I found out about this place for housing students and tourists so I bunked there for the night. The next morning several students asked where I was headed next. I told them that I was just traveling to see the sights and eventually heading for the Grand Canyon. They were all from other countries and their desire was to go to Mesa Verde National Park. I told them I would take them to be a witness to them of Jesus Christ love to them and one lady was Jewish. When we reached the top of this lookout type mountain you could see for more than twenty miles.

I remember there were caves and they were interested in Indian artifacts, so I went with them for the day to continue to show God's love to them. They all split up from me except the Jewish lady and she was very intrigued by my stories of faith. At the Grand Canyon site, I accidentally locked us out of my rental car. So, I was attempting to take a coat hanger to open the door, but with all my efforts, I failed. I told her that I was going to pray and almost immediately the latch popped up on its own. I was amazed, but she was totally amazed.

I had rented a cabin at the Grand Canyon for a few days and I saw the whole south side of the canyon and I couldn't get enough of it. One day, I rented a small airplane to fly over the Canyon and the pilot was a born again Christian. So we were rejoicing and fellow shipping, but the passengers didn't seem to have as much fun.

One morning, I started out about 5 a.m. and was going down the eleven- mile trip down into the Canyon; I got there about noon. I played some horse shoes with some new friends then ate my lunch and headed back up the canyon which wasn't as easy as coming down. It was beginning to get dark and I had quite a bit to go, and I didn't want to stay all night on the very small trail going up. My legs were really worn out so I took the time to pray and I was able to make it to the top. I was tired, but rejoicing that God had given me His Strength to make it all the way.

I went to other places like the Painted Desert, Volcano Park and Meteor Valley where a meteor hit earth years ago. I went many other places, but I was always fortunate to find a church to attend the whole time. I remember my money was very low on funds and I went to church the last Sunday before it was time to leave. God told me with the little I had, to give five dollars that morning and went again that evening and God said to give another five. I have never questioned God, so I obeyed. I was taking the rental car back and just before I turned it in, I had to fill up the tank and it was my last ten-dollar traveler's check with a five- dollar bill. I thank God I had just enough, I was watching my money very carefully. I gave the attendant the ten-dollar traveler's check with the five and no sooner than I reached for the door the attendant motioned back to me. He said: "Don't you want your change from the twenty-dollar traveler's check?" I knew I had just given him a ten and he showed me it was a twenty! What God did was give me back that last ten dollars that he asked me to give to be able to eat and unbelievably changed the ten-dollar traveler's check into a twenty.

One other time back in Tampa, I lost a company money order, or so I thought. My wife (ex-wife) said she found it in my pants in the washed laundry shredded in pieces. I told the clerk where I had bought it and she told me: "If you could find a piece that says $50.00, I will give you another money order." When we looked through the shreds we actually found a shred that said $50.00 and it was no bigger than that figure. I returned it and she could hardly believe it herself. I know nothing is Impossible with God. No wonder God says that obedience is better than sacrifice.

Faith Adventures Episode 44
Can We Do What Jesus Said-Turn the Other Cheek?

Now this is a very controversial Scripture, when Messiah Jesus told us to turn the other cheek. Most of us as believers, don't believe it is possible to do this very thing that Jesus said for us to do. Matthew 5:39 NASB But I say to you, do not resist an evil person, but whoever slaps you on your right cheek, turn the other to him also. He has told us in accordance to His Word that we can do all things through Him who strengthens us. Most believers don't see that He can strengthen us in matters such as this?

I would from time to time stop in and talk to this gal in a convenience store while she was waiting on customers. This one particular night I believe God led me to say to this sixty-two-year-old man something needed. I asked him if he knew Christ as his personal Savior? He responded and said he had been a chaplain in the U.S. Navy for twenty-five years. I responded back and said that you didn't answer my question. I think he got a little bit upset over the question. He told me that I had a big mouth in speaking what I was speaking. I told him I'm speaking in accordance to what Jesus said. He responded and said that He had a big mouth also. I felt upset and hurting inside with this comment. Apparently, I didn't show it because of his response. He told me that he was sixty-two and that he would take me out and beat my butt! I told him that I was glad to meet him, even though he put his fists right under my chin touching me. I told him that Jesus loves him and that I would be praying for him. I was only in my late thirties and the shape I was in, I would have taken him up on his offer. What would this have of accomplished? I said to myself this would accomplish absolutely nothing. There was no doubt he had other bouts throughout his life, in my observance in how easily he got upset. I believe that he would never forget the response that Jesus demonstrated through me to him!

Now some time later, there was a situation that happened to me by another co-worker, Wayne. I knew I was in the right so I told him that he was a liar. I quickly learned that day that was not the choicest words to use towards another man. He began to plow into me and like a boxer, hit me in my right eye and the blood came bursting out! I didn't turn my cheek exactly like the Bible says. I turned around after being battered a few times and he continued to pound on my back. As he was walking away, I shouted out to him. I love you because of Christ love in me in spite of all you have done to me. It is only by God's strength that anyone of us can respond in such love.

Now I'm still bleeding and have to finish my route deliveries, trying my best to cover up. One other Vendor saw what had happened to me and asked what happened? Now this man wanted to have nothing to do with me before, much less talk to me. He asked me why did I let Wayne do this to me? I simply answered because I believe what the Bible tells me to do. Sometimes we can be blessed in doing what God's Word says. Other times we might have to suffer for Christ's sake and learn the fellowship of Christ's sufferings. He could hardly believe what I was saying, but I believe it was a powerful witness to him, probably he had never heard something like that before. I opened up to a Scripture during this time in my little New Testament. I carried it everywhere I went and God ministered to me powerfully.

I finished my work that day and when I went into the agency, I begin to get the blame for what Wayne had done to me. This Scripture that God gave me earlier prepared me even for that. Do we take it patiently when accused wrongly? 1Peter 2:20 NASB For what credit is there if, when you sin and are harshly treated, you endure it with patience? But if you do what is right and suffer for it you patiently endure it, this finds favor with God.

It was only three days later and my eye was healed up completely and many could hardly believe it. The Bible says not to strike the anointed. I never once thought to get revenge back to this person. My thoughts were Romans 12:9 "Vengeance is Mine, says the Lord, I will repay!" God proves Himself to be true over and over again. This man Wayne was out of work after this for nearly a year because his back had gone out on him and I heard he couldn't do anything, but just lay there for the majority of that year!

This dream I had comes to mind to end this episode. In this dream, God was showing me the revelation of Luke 10:19. He has given us power to tread on serpents and scorpions and power and authority over all the authority of the enemy and nothing shall by any means hurt you. In this dream, I was out witnessing in a bowling alley and I was going next door to an empty building and someone followed me. This person had a fairly large pair of scissors and was stabbing me in the back of my head continuously! Obviously, I was bleeding profusely and the assailant was on top of me pinning me down. Somehow, no doubt by God's Strength I was able to pin him down. I told him that if he didn't get right with God, that a fiery hell would be worse than to him than this experience.

I arose and some doctors approached me in amazement. They were talking to one another about how there was no hope for me survive this ordeal. In response, I said to them that if God wants me to continue to preach this Gospel, I will live to do that very thing. One other thing is very important to note is that I experienced no pain all throughout this dream. I know that we can experience pain in dreams so this was God speaking through this dream of His protection over my life.

Faith Adventures Episode 45
Miraculous Love Brings Miraculous Deliverance

I was attending First Nazarene Church in Tampa, sometime after my wife left me. I was always looking to disciple or mentor because of this calling He had placed on my life. I met this younger girl new in the faith, Joni and began ministering to her. There should have been a woman to be doing this very thing. There was not a one in a fairly large church to love and minister to her. She had never known or experienced this Christ kind of love coming from a man. She poured out her life to me and it was something no girl should have had to experience. She told me that men would come over to her apartment and just use and abuse her and she actually thought this was the way life was. Her natural father had begun this vicious cycle from the time she was twelve years of age. He continued this ungodly act for many years and she told me he would actually break in her apartment to do so. This man also was a prominent member in the church. She was now at the age of about thirty and these things were still happening. My heart poured out to her in compassion. Right or wrong as it may have been, I became like her protector. I would go over her place prayerfully to show her how God would protect her from all these evil men, and put my life on the line probably many times. Even her father knew he would be exposed if he kept doing these things.

God kept me pure through it all even though she desired me. She desired the love of God she saw in me and I give God Glory she saw Christ's love through me. In the process of time I discovered she would daily listen to Pink Floyd's album, Dark Side of the Moon. One day I was reading the lyrics of the song, The Lunatic. I took notice that the lyrics were saying: "the blade sprang up," and I knew by the

Spirit that this very quote was in the Bible. Remember this, because this is something very important pertaining to her life. One night, I received a call from her and, I could tell she was very terrified of something that just happened. She told me her father had just been shot by a man attempting to steal her car at her mother's house. I told her I was coming over right away. When I arrived, the police had already left. The family asked me to go to their neighbor's house to bring a rookie policeman there. To this day, I don't know why they asked me to do this. We were coming back to her home and took notice that her car door was partially open. She had assured us that it was completely locked up. I suggested that we check it out. I opened the car door and the man actually had come back to the scene of the crime. I heard the rookie say: He's got a gun as he ran into the house and locked me out. I stood there in the power of God's Spirit looking this man straight in the eyes telling him that he had no hope outside of Jesus Christ, and continued by God's Spirit to speak to him regarding his soul. I had no fear whatsoever the whole time. I watched as he ran away.

I walked into the house and everyone was so afraid that I had to dial the number for the police and I had the peace of God mightily upon me. The police arrived and was asking the others, who had spoken to him last? They never bothered to ask about the fact I spoke to him. When they approached, me they asked me where I had last seen him. When I told them about everything that happened, they were all wagging their heads in unbelief. I know God had me say this in His Spirit directly to them: "You will find him within the hour, but you will not harm him." They returned within the hour and the Sergeant was sharing with us what happened. This was not the regular routine of doing things, I assure you. He said that they had caught up with him and there were seven of them surrounding him with guns. He said something happened that never he had experienced. We were all ready to shoot him when he reached in his pocket, but something stopped us from shooting him, and no doubt killing him. I responded what you and your fellow officers experienced was the Power of God. He couldn't argue with that because of what he saw with his own eyes.

I saw a love that only Christ could give a person through Joni like I had never seen before. God truly had put this love in her heart for her father. We all prayed for him and of course, the assailant, and at this point her father had not changed. What love only God can bestow upon a person He bestowed upon Joni.

From observing Joni for some time, God was showing me we would be dealing with the demonic realm. One night I was in her home with another believer and I was asking her about a jewelry box that was given to her by a friend in Colorado. This friend was involved with witchcraft and I observed a white powder around this box. I told Joni I was taking this box because I believe it was causing her continual sickness. As I was traveling home in separate vehicles from my friend I sensed an influence of sickness going through my body and my friend sensed heaviness on his chest. God was showing us something. When I got home I decided to leave it outside under my mobile home and put anointing oil all over this box and prayed. Joni called me about four hours later wanting me to bring her box back. I was reluctant to do this, but when I went to retrieve this jewelry box it had disappeared and we never saw it again.

On another night, a brother and I took her to a church which was known for the deliverance of people. Joni began acting up, because the demon was manifesting itself. The Associate Pastor heard the commotion and told us to get her out of the church. I responded, could we not take her to a back room for deliverance? He said, No.

We took her out to the parking lot and we begin to pray over her for deliverance. This same pastor said for us to completely leave the premises. We went further away and continued to pray. We were not going to give up that night until we saw her deliverance. We had been praying for some time and God by His Spirit had me say; that's it, the blade sprang up, remembering the lyrics to the Pink Floyd song. The demons begin to speak out of her repeatedly: I am the lunatic I am the lunatic! We knew God was delivering her. I just began to thank Jesus for her deliverance over and over again many more times than what the demons had professed.

Some young people were coming out into the parking lot and came over and also were praying with us. They said they were going home to get rid of all their rock and roll albums. They also had experienced a real deliverance! Isn't it amazing, how when it comes to real deliverance how Satan will show up even in a pastor to stop what God wants to do!

Faith Adventures Episode 46
Infatuation Can Take You Down the Wrong Path

This is something I experienced that I should warn many of us; and that is infatuation. Thank God my love for my Messiah was stronger than anything or anyone could be in my life. I don't believe I knew what real love in a relationship was because God definitely didn't put it in my first marriage together. This is an unbelievable experience and will hopefully minister to the reader. One evening, I was watching a Christian television network in Canada and I saw this gal, beautiful in every way as a Christian woman singer. God was using her mightily to minister to others and I liked what I was seeing. She was so precious and special in the Lord in every way. I felt like I was falling in love all over again and I never felt this way in a long time.

I decided to do what I thought would be the impossible. I called the hotel where she was staying to tell her how precious she was in ministering, and that I had watched her on tv. In our conversation, she told me she would be visiting her aunt in Lakeland. I don't know why, but I asked the telephone number and address so that I could call her and maybe send her something. She actually gave me all this information. At this time in my life I was very vulnerable and if someone had given me some prophetic word, I would have probably made more of a fool of myself.

I was soaring in my spirit because I thought I was in love, or was going to be. I could hardly believe this was happening and thinking that God has to be in this. I sent her some flowers because I started thinking again: God must be in this. I got her return call on my message machine. She thanked me for the flowers; I soared once again.

Now I am really soaring, about to hit the ceiling and I played her voice over maybe a hundred times. I didn't know what was going on at this time. I only knew at this time I wanted to get to know this wonderful woman of God. Sometimes we can get off course in our thinking because of the way that God seems to be orchestrating this whole thing. I decided I was going to take a drive over into her area of town and give her a call to hopefully be able to meet her in person. Her aunt had answered the phone and asked if I would like to come over and wait for her return. I said yes ma'am, I would like to do that if you think it will be alright. She assured me that was not a problem.

Sometimes we can pursue someone in a godly way taking our own initiative, in making something happen on our own. At some point, I was still soaring inside about to meet the girl of my dreams because I had just about given up on something like this happening. I was as nervous as a jay bird, but knocked on her door and her aunt was very nice. She came home shortly and entered the room I was waiting in. I was doing everything I knew to do in holding back my emotions. The room we entered into was her piano room where she had written all of her songs. She told me about a song which happened to be my favorite Scripture and sang it for me and I told her how much I loved her ministry. I took notice that there were some dead flowers on top of her piano. She mentioned to me that they were the flowers I had sent. I was probably there an hour or so but loving every minute of it.

Well I knew that I would never get a chance again to probably see her, so I asked if we could get together at another time. She told me that she was engaged to someone else and then I could hear my heart drop! I still had her address so I decided to write her shortly after I moved to Colorado for Bible College, but I never received a letter in return. I concentrated now on what God was calling me to and kept very busy in ministry and never thought much again about her.

Four years later after I graduated from Bible College with a B average, I was visiting a few of my colleagues to be a part of something God had started with them, because they had left the college the year before. There was Big John and Patricia and we were taking part in what God was doing at Patricia's church. God had used me to bring someone to her church and this has always been a thrill for me to this day. This may have been God showing me that I was called to be an evangelist, not a pastor, which I discovered soon after Bible College.

John and I got a motel together and one evening I turned on the television and there she was again on television. ,Apparently, I had mentioned to my brother sometime about this wonderful Christian girl. He commented: "No wonder you wanted to be with her," because he could see she would be a great catch. Now I would like to speak a word of caution to the men or women that are presently married. It could be the same thing would happen to you, especially if the spouse you are with presently was not God chosen and God spoken into your life. Understand that an infatuation type love is not Agape Love. What happened to me over five years ago was beginning to happen all over again. This was infatuation at its highest peak and I couldn't believe this was happening all over again.

When I saw she was going to be in my town, Tampa at the time, I thought once again of buying and sending her some flowers, but God stopped me by speaking great volume into my life concerning a relationship. I soon realized this when she didn't even remember me and that had to be God's doing also. God said to me: you desire a good thing my son, but I have someone picked out for you that is so much better for you which I have designed for your life. It was God's voice that stopped me in my tracks to keep me from making a fool of myself later.

The point I'm trying to make here is that we need to always be tuned in, listening to God's voice in all matters, especially the most important decisions we will make in our lives. I knew God had someone specially designed for me because He told me and He has never failed me! You will read about the wife the Lord designed for my life in the upcoming Faith Adventures.

Faith Adventures Episode 47
God's Deliverance from Rock and Roll Music

Now I would like to talk about the convictions that have developed in my life since coming to Christ. God put such a love in my heart that it pounded for others to know Him. We as sinners that have come out of that lifestyle, we still haven't seen the reality of becoming clean before our Lord. The drinking wasn't much of a problem because the only reason I did this was because I was a big part of the nightclub scene. This means I went out to pick up women and I can barely today remember a lot of them. So putting away the alcohol was not a problem with me. The problem even as a believer was rationalizing my marijuana usage. I wasn't partaking of this in the same manner because thank God, He had taken me out of that environment. My favorite rock group Ten Years Later was coming into town for a concert and I decided to go to try to reach my favorite artist for Christ. God only knows by my efforts what happened. I heard and read later that this man had some kind of conversion experience prior to the concert. I had a special shirt made up with the lead guitarist's name of group and band. In these atmospheres, which I had experienced many times I had a desire to meet these rock musicians, but it never seemed to happen. On this occasion the lead guitarist saw my shirt and commented, "You have my shirt on!" There was a time when I would have been thrilled to hear that, but I kept reminding myself or God reminding me of why I came there? This was because I wanted him to know my Lord. The atmosphere was so full of marijuana and I think I just took one tote that got me little high. It was through this experience of God's conviction that I realized I cannot do this again.

One other time, a gal was cutting my hair while I was still married and offered me marijuana. I knew if I started doing this with her that I would be doing other things that would be displeasing to God. For some reason, I still had some around the house so the Holy Spirit was convicting me to flush it down the toilet and I never touched it again after that day. Now Rock music was something I had made a god of, because it was my escape from circumstances in my family the early years of my life. This is something that you might say was ingrained in my life; I did not see how this had affected my thinking even as a Christian.

I really liked this one particular evangelist because many of his messages had really spoke to me. This one particular day, he was speaking about the rock music and how it has affected so many young people's lives. I really don't remember what the evangelist was saying to this day. I do remember the response of the young people bringing their rock music albums up front to destroy all of them and this spoke to me powerfully. I gathered all of my collection of $5000.00 worth of Rock music and took them outside, to get a hammer to break them up and destroy them. This truly was the conviction of the Holy Spirit upon me to do such a radical thing!

Many young people today are talking about radical Christianity, but I don't hear anything going on in our day like this for young people to turn away from their sins. As I was breaking up these albums, spare none, young people in my neighborhood wanted me to give them to them. I told them no and I would not be responsible for the blood of your souls on my conscience. In the book of Acts 19:17-20, the Christians did a similar thing and the fear of God came upon the church. In verse 17, this became known to all, both Jews and Greeks, who lived in Ephesus and fear fell upon them all and the name of the Lord Jesus was being magnified. In verse 18, many of those who had believed kept coming, confessing and disclosing their practices. In verse 19, many of those who practiced magic brought their books together and began burning them in the sight of everyone and they counted up the price of them and found it fifty thousand pieces of silver. In verse 20: "So the word of the Lord was growing mightily and prevailing."

It was because of the thing they attempted to do, the casting out of demonic forces. Today we are not casting them out, but are inviting them in and now that we have let them in we can't find our way out. In most professing Christians, the enemy has set up shop in our minds and we are doing the enemies business, not God's anymore, in most circles. In the Epistle of John, it says if we sin, that is come into a practice of sin, that we are serving the devil by sinning in this manner. Far too many of us have thrown the Holy Spirit out and not invited him in! The problem is that most of us don't even know it has happened! Look at Sampson and His sins that brought him to this very place.

I had just had one of the most exhilarating experiences in watching God work in a tremendous manner being led to the Black Sabbath Rock concert, and to see the effects that prayer and faith came to pass within two hours after prayer.

I wanted for God to use me once again in this manner, so instead of hearing God on this matter; I called to find out when the next popular group was coming to town and I couldn't wait to see what God was going to do next. This time, I went all alone, probably not thinking in my excitement. When I arrived, the concert was not on. Apparently, I was given the wrong information of their scheduled concert. I didn't bother to find out the day the other group was coming. I asked what was going on, and I was told it was free to see this faith healer. I would have never gone out of my way to see anyone like this. I thought, I'm here; I might as well go in and I walked in, and the place was set up just like any other conference meeting. I saw a table full of Bibles for sale and books of course, but I happened to have my own Bible. So I went into the meeting and sat down and took the time to observe my surroundings. As I looked around I didn't see any Bibles. My first thought was: Why did they come here? Then the faith healer began to speak about some people getting saved and I had just seen my pastor's son get saved and I was responding in my amen corner. I looked around at all the crowd and no one was responding positively. Again, my thoughts were: Why did they come here, and what is it they were looking for?

Now remember I'm a fairly young believer at this time and didn't know what to expect. All of a sudden as soon as the preacher started talking about healing testimonies, the place went wild. They could have matched up in their excitement to a super bowl crowd. "Again the thought came to me: Why they are here? The preacher begin to name different diseases and infirmities and they would by groups and individuals stand up when asked. God began to remind me of the story of how the people in John 2 were following the Messiah just for the miracles. When you are in a setting like this, it's vitally important to know the Scriptures and listen to what the Holy Spirit is saying. These people were not committed believers. Messiah Jesus said in John 2:23-25, He was in Jerusalem at the Passover in the feast day many believed in His name, when they saw the miracles which he did.

This Word "believe" in the original language means that they only believed; to the extent in what they were seeing like is the case with many still today, sad to say. Jesus did not commit himself unto them because he knew all men, needed not that any should testify of man for he knew what was in man. This is the Biblical evidence that if we draw near to Him, He in turn will draw near unto us. How can we take the word of a preacher that tells us it's all grace and nothing we have to do on our part.. Paul said that we need to work out our own salvation with fear and trembling.

Then God spoke something to me about this whole meeting and from what God said this could pertain to thousands of others that have been held in this manner. God said: When these people came seeking miracles and really don't have a heart to seek Me, when they receive they are led into deception in the sense they keep coming back. The Lord also said that: Each time they come back many times for the same healings, they get worse and worse each time. There was a man Messiah told this John 8:11: NASB "Afterward Jesus found him in the temple and said to him Behold you have become well; do not sin anymore, so that nothing worse happens to you."

There are two things we all can learn out of this if we are willing to listen.

1. Don't go into Satan's territory unless you know God has spoken to you on this matter, with confirmation, because the results will not be the same. In a future Faith Adventures, I will tell of another matter to display this truth. I would also say: Stop going to man because by going to man you are looking at men too much and they can become your idol.
2. We don't need to go to a faith healer to receive our healings and deliverances. We can pray individually to God or the best way is to present all of our concerns to our pastor to present all are concerns to a local Body for prayer.

Faith Adventures Episode 48
Deliverance of Black Sabbath Worshippers

I'm still in Tampa and oddly enough, God was speaking to me about going to a "Black Sabbath" concert. Shortly after this, I heard an advertisement on the radio about this event coming to Lakeland. I believed this was the Lord confirming to me that He wanted me to go to minister to the people that Christ is the answer. I asked my church Body to pray for me, because this was the devil's territory we were about to invade. I didn't know how many followers of Christ were going to show up to pray. I was trying to call my good friend Joe that had been very supportive with me in many other endeavors of ministry in the past years. I knew I could count on Joe showing up and when I arrived, no one else was in sight as far as I could see. I prayed and had the confidence that God had sent me on this mission. I was thinking, I'm all alone and then it came to me that Jesus was here with me and working. I knew He would show up because He always does. I wasn't led at this place to give out tracks of the Gospel, but just to speak His Words of Life and Truth. I had brought a license plate and just held it up and it said "Jesus is the Answer!"

Most just passed by hurrying into the concert, not paying much attention to me, but a few stopped and we spoke. One of the security guards was trying to get me to leave by trying to throw fear into me. He told me that there was another man last week doing what I was doing and someone hit him over the head and they took him away in an ambulance. I responded: I don't know why that person came, but I know why I came. I came because God sent me here tonight, and he walked away in disgust.

Then I had a few well-meaning Christians come and try to tell me that I was going about this in the wrong way. Instead of me arguing I suggested that we pray about this matter. Their ministry was to give out tracts, but I saw them rushed by the security guards off the property. I never tried to tell them what I thought, that they may be going about this in the wrong way. I just prayed to let God have His way and about all the followers of the rock group "Black Sabbath" had all went into the concert. One member of another group that professed to know Christ stopped, and God spoke through me and said: "If you really believe then you will do as Jesus said that you will keep all His commandments." He responded in a very hesitating manner, and said, "I keep all His commandments." I'm still alone after all this time, so I decided to walk around and possibly find my friend. It was much to my surprise that I had not only found him but about thirty others ready to pray and do battle. It would be an understatement to say I was really excited.

We began to pray and the Spirit of the Lord came upon me mightily and I was praying that the spiritual walls would fall at this concert. Also, that these followers would see Satan because he would have to reveal himself to them in some way. We were praying in the analogy of how Joshua and his people prayed and the Walls of Jericho fell done within. That was our prayer, that God would show these followers through their inner selves which God has put within all of us. So then we begin to put feet to our prayers and we begin to walk around this huge Lakeland Center and our prayer, just as Joshua's people did was to march around seven times. We had gone around only two times and these believers begin to leave our group in this march. I asked them: ""What they were doing?"" I also said: ""Are we going to believe what we prayed or not?"" They said they didn't feel that this was right and went on their way. I remember one gal marched up to five times and she left also. Now it was my friend Joe that stuck with me through the whole march.

Just as we finished seconds later, these Black Sabbath followers had come out screaming that they could see Satan. This is not what happens in rock concerts. They stay until the very last tune is played. I should know; I saw many of the greats play in concert stadiums and arenas. Remember before Christ, I made a god out of Rock and Roll music. Many of these believers that had left the march were still waiting around and begin to minister to these early departures of men and women. Now my friend, who supported me through this whole thing was a strong believer of being led by the spirit to do anything. He said: If another one comes out, I believe the Lord wants us to go in. So another man came out and we entered this concert and that's something I never planned to happen. We also prayed that this group would not for some reason, be able to make an animal sacrifice and God stopped that from happening also.

We entered into the side of the main stage and we could see the crowd of followers worshipping with all their might. One man said he was so glad for having this experience, that it gave him a new burden for souls for God's Kingdom. I was standing there also, with a Bible in one hand and the Jesus is the answer license plate in the other. I sensed a demonic oppression all over me, something that I had never experienced as a believer before.

God was saying to me that I was not dealing with just a few demons, but armies of demons that surround these groups. One thing I learned from this and another experience I had later during my Bible College days in Colorado Springs Colorado; we don't go into the enemy's territory, unless we know it's Him directing us to do so. God, willing you will hear about this upcoming Faith Adventure.

Faith Adventures Episode 49
The Power Of Prayer With Faith

Can we all remember when God was putting it on our hearts to pray for usually many people that God would by His Spirit would do this very thing? This would usually happen to me in the early morning hours on my way to work. This was when I was tired or frustrated and just plain didn't have any desire to pray for others. This is what you might call a battle with the flesh and the spirit. My spirit inside of me was speaking in greater volume than my flesh! My spirit or God speaking within me was revealing to me that without some kind of commitment to prayer, I would not be able to overcome the flesh. This is what prompted me to read and learn more about prayer especially for others.

We started the prayer meetings every Saturday evening at Tampa First Nazarene Church starting about eight and going until sometimes twelve midnight. This began from this book, Power of Prayer. I was reading and really meditating about the fact all of the great revivals began with prayer. There were true stories about even when a few came together for prayer, God brought great revival to many cities and even little towns. God was beginning to birth within me and others a vision for revival in our churches.

In these special prayer meetings that were prompted by God's Spirit, God used a very powerful book I believe, by R. A. Torrey about prayer and how believers would meet on a night where no activity was going on in the church. These believers determined themselves to come together to pour out their hearts to God crying out for real Revival. It was just a few of us that gathered consistently to pray for our church, to come to see revival in us as well as them.

At some point, I was reading the Scriptures in John 13 regarding Messiah Jesus washing the disciples' feet. It dawned on me by the Holy Spirit that Jesus never washed anyone else's feet except the disciples, in accordance to the Scriptures. In verse 14 this says, "If your Master have washed your feet you should wash one another's feet." In verse 17 the Lord said that we would be happy if we did these things. God's revelation came to me that we are to wash the believer's feet in which we have made an impact on their lives. There were believers that Christ through me affected for God's Kingdom in becoming disciples.

These were some of the believers that had joined me in these earlier meetings. These few that were gathered together with me in prayer were the ones that God wanted this to happen with, because certain believers didn't show up this particular evening. God was saying through others, that God never meant for them to be there because of what God was showing me. Now they came back after this for us to continue to pray that God pour down revival on us. The Revelation came to me was that the only feet Messiah Jesus ever washed was His disciples. This I believed strongly was pure revelation from the Hand of our Father.

So, that particular night I believe God was leading me to do what His Word was saying for me to do. Remember our Master said: "If I then your Lord and Master, have washed your feet you also ought to wash one another's feet to His disciples." I prepared a basin of water and towels just before everyone entered that night. I began to wash each one's feet one by one and some responded back and washed mine also. I took noticed that a few washed my feet with such love in return for what God was doing in them. We all experienced such joy and it was a different kind of joy that only God could pour forth on us all that we would never forget how that God came mightily upon us.

At this time period something that happened that never happened to this holiness church since its beginning. We started a Dynamics of Discipleship program by Don Wellman. I had been thinking about this for some time lately and couldn't come up with this programs title, and as I was writing it came to me miraculously. It was very exciting to see that there were over one hundred participants and that most had gone the distance of the yearly course. God was doing something in this church that never happened before and probably hasn't happened since. You could hear the testimonies week after week what God was doing and many were being tested also. To my remembrance, now there were times on a Sunday morning God came in a powerful manner. Prior to this, I approached our pastor and asked him the question. "Why don't we have altar calls on Sunday morning?" He answered probably because we have been caught up in tradition. Only on Sunday evenings were these more spiritual times taking place.

I remember a time when what I call Resurrection Sunday (Easter) that many were responding to the message and pouring out their hearts to God. I also distinctly remember this 25 year veteran missionary going to the altar and crying out to God in repentance that she was dry and needed God's refreshing so and God came mightily upon her and her testimony rang throughout the whole congregation. There were two responses that I was hearing. The people that remained sitting in their pews visiting or otherwise, would comment: "What is happening in this place and I never heard or experienced such things," so they remained seated, but God was putting them in awe. On the other hand, there were people probably observing only and they would see these things happening and would respond; it's all part of the act. One young believer was stunned by their response I heard later. I responded that that was good. She responded in amazement of my response and asked me, why? I told her because this can show them where they are at spiritually, and if they think about it long enough it can bring change to their hearts. This is what real revival does. Revival reveals the hearts of men to themselves and that can bring the change around depending on them and our prayers on behalf of them. I just wish I could have recorded all the testimonies we would hear Sunday after Sunday of hearts being changed for the Kingdom of God's work. I remember it was on a Sunday evening everyone in the entire church was kneeling before God. We were all crying out for God's mercy to be upon us in a true godly repentance.

I also remember a new pastor that had one of the largest congregations in Florida. He was testifying that he visited a holiness church in a revival meeting and saw all the people on their knees crying out to God. This experience prompted him to put altars into his church, which became the biggest church in Florida at the time. W.A. Criswell visited some holiness revival meetings prior to this time. God placed on his heart to place altars in many Baptist churches to this day.

As by the Holy Spirit's remembrance all these things have been written. These Faith Adventures and so much more put me in mind of something God said John 21:25 NASB ""And there were also many other things which Jesus did, which if they were written in detail, I suppose that even the world itself would not contain the books that would be written" I'm not saying my life is likened to His. I am saying that I can't remember it all, to put it all in writing the things that Christ has done through me. God willing, I will be writing for some time to come. As I always say to God be the Glory for what He has done.

Faith Adventures Episode 50
God's Faith Assignment-Bible College

By this time in my walk with the Lord, I had experienced so much in the miraculous and the unexplainable. Matthew 5:8 states: "Blessed are you that hunger and thirst after Righteousness for you shall be filled." Our church had just experienced real revival and at that time I was blessed beyond measure. When people would ask me how I was doing I would say, if it was going to get any better, that I would not be able to stand it. I would also say that my physical body can't keep up with what God's spirit was doing within me.

God worked out everything to go to Bible College including the support of my church. When I began to ponder over the thoughts of going to Bible College it kind of frightened me. This is because at the time when I attended high school a graduate only needed 17 credits to graduate. And I received a whopping 17 and half credits! As you can see, I barely made it through. God came and spoke to me at this same time period. First He said: My son, you can only do so much. I couldn't disagree with that truth because I knew I was limited. Then God said I want to send you that I may use you that I may do so much more. This is the reason I went to college. It was like another faith assignment that God had spoken into my life.

In September 1984, I was preparing to go to Bible College. This particular college did not teach that the church has replaced Israel. On the contrary, the professors said that we don't know the New Testament without first knowing the Old Testament. I experienced good biblical foundational principles in accordance to the Whole Counsel of God; the entire inspired Word of God. At this time I had sold just about everything I owned. This event happened on the

Friday, just before I was to leave. I had just awakened from a nap. As soon as I arose I began to experience visual swaying inside my home as well as outside. I approached my neighbor and asked: "What was happening to me?" He replied in saying that I had equilibrium imbalance. He said that was a form of severe ear infection. I did not know what to do. He replied and said: "I should call Albertsons to obtain ear drops." I called and they replied that I had to set up an appointment with a doctor. I told them I don't have time for that so I'm taking this thing to God, my healer. I was already pressed for time and literally had no time.

I decided my only recourse was to take this matter to God and God alone. I began to pray in faith, praise Him, dance before Him and just simply believe for His miraculous healing touch and it happened within the hour. I believe this was an all out attack from the enemy to stop me from fulfilling what God had called me to.

On that very weekend I decided God wanted me to testify on Sunday morning of what God had done to give him all the glory. God was having me give the devil a black eye, so to speak. God had me to tell it just the way it happened. Just as I was ready to be seated, the same symptoms began to come upon me. I told the enemy that I was not receiving any of this. I arrived at Bible College in the mountains, where there was quite an altitude change. The whole time I attended the college, there was never ever any such thing and to this day there is nothing in that manner that has happened. All I can do is give what's due to Him all the Glory, all the praise and all the honor due to Him and Him Alone. God willing, volume two of Faith Adventures will be published, my Bible College days.

THANKS FOR YOUR TIME- YOUR TIME IS VALUABLE

My name is Evangelist Norman Sergent and I graduated from Nazarene Bible College. I'm an Evangelist that ministers to believers, teaching the message of God's Kingdom, to encourage, educate, disciple, and counsel Facebook followers.
Website:

My email is faithadventures7@gmail.com.
My phone number for any response to my book is
407-489-5679, or 407-495-5596.
I'm in Orlando, Florida, the Norman Sergent Facebook page.

If you would like me to come speak at your church, contact me or for any other reason I will be available.